PARTNERS IN CREATION

Stewardship for Pastor and People

by
Ronald D. Petry

The Brethren Press, Elgin, Illinois

Library of Congress Cataloging in Publication Data

Petry, Ronald D   1934—
    Partners in creation.

    Bibliography: p.
    1. Stewardship, Christian.   I. Title.
BV772.P45   248′.6   79-21770
ISBN 0-87178-688-5

Published by The Brethren Press, Elgin, Illinois 60120

Partners in Creation

Stewardship for Pastor and People

TABLE OF CONTENTS

PART II — STEWARDSHIP: THE PASTOR'S ROLE

APPENDIXES

PREFACE

This study was conceived from its earliest stages as a project that should be of practical value to persons in training for ministry, those already engaged in pastoral leadership, and other congregational leaders in stewardship. Whether this objective has been achieved is a matter for each reader to evaluate. It should be clear, however, that this value was in the forefront of my thinking from beginning to end.

Persons who have participated in the development of the study include Mildred Etter Heckert, Ralph G. McFadden, Joel K. Thompson, and Ann Marie Walz. These persons have been generous with their time in numerous meetings and in the reading and critiquing of the manuscript. Members of the Bethany Theological Seminary faculty have offered valuable suggestions which are reflected at many points throughout the study. Warm appreciation is expressed to Dale W. Brown, Estella B. Horning, and Byron P. Royer for their thoughtful inquiries, probings, and steady support. A word of gratitude is recorded here also to Graydon F. Snyder, dean of the Seminary and the one who planted the seed for this study.

Finally, the able secretarial assistance of Mary Henry and Wanda Sturdevant is gratefully acknowledged.

Ronald D. Petry

INTRODUCTION

The purpose of this study is to offer a theologically based guide for stewardship in the local church. The primary intended audience is pastors in training and pastors already in service, as well as lay stewardship leaders. Others may read these pages and benefit from them, but it was for the purpose of strengthening the hand of professional church leaders especially that this study was prepared.

Research indicates that most theological seminaries in North America do not include courses in Christian stewardship as a part of pastoral training. This was found to be the case in 60 percent of the seminaries responding to a 1976 survey conducted by the Commission on Stewardship of the National Council of Churches.[1] The study also reflects this writer's conviction and that of numerous colleagues that stewardship is an area that can be slighted only to the church's detriment through the inadequate preparation of pastors.

The material in these pages arises from the belief that the pastor has a vital role to fill in local church stewardship development. It arises, further, from the belief that the pastor needs both to address the concerns of stewardship from the standpoint of faith and to be a practitioner of the stewardship which that faith calls forth. These pages also point to the need for strong lay participation and leadership in the ministry of Christian stewardship.

Many of the ideas presented here have been tested and refined in various settings. The chapters in Part I, for example, were developed originally in somewhat different form as the outline for a stewardship course conducted by the author at the Highland Avenue Church of the Brethren, Elgin Illinois. Part II picks up on practical experience in ministry both as a pastor and as a national staff person with stewardship responsibilities.

The author's hope is that seminarians will be stimulated to do careful thought and further study as a result of this reading, and that they will find excitement in the theology and practice of

Christian stewardship. The hope for pastors us that they, too, will be drawn into further dialogue concerning effective leadership in the church and their own deeper commitment as stewards of God. The hope for lay leaders who read this book is that they will grow in their understanding of biblical stewardship as well as in their readiness to make stewardship an ongoing congregational priority.

PART I

A FAITH VIEW

CHAPTER
1

CHRIST IS THE
CENTER OF LIFE

The assertion that Christ is the center of life may strike some readers as being quite out of touch with reality. Evidence to support their reaction is readily available, as indicated by: a national economy based on manufactured desires and needs that appeal to vanity and depend heavily on planned obsolescence, a world arms race that makes the business of destruction one of the most profitable enterprises around, a multiple choice of idolatries done up in multi-media splendor.

In the midst of all the things and the unbelievable abundance that surround persons in the western world, in the presence of great wealth and mountainous waste, it is not surprising that some should consider as slightly empty-headed the claim that Christ is the center of life. Indeed, most of what life is made of, or much of what is done with it, seems to fly in the face of the claim we are addressing and stands in direct opposition to it.

Theological Foundations
The fact, though, if one dare speak of fact in matters of faith, is that the ultimate meaning of Christ would be utterly destroyed if the revelation in him had very little or nothing to do with persons caught up in the maddening world of the latter fifth of the twentieth century. The assumption made here is that we share a common faith in Christ; a faith that has implications for our lives

and the lives of all who truly hear the gospel. Though to some persons the gospel may seem far from their daily needs and concerns, the testimony of others is that it is closer to them than breathing.

The good news—the *best* news—is that we are never alone, left to our own devices. This is not to imply that by some special decree there is a sort of divine secret protection given to each of the faithful. There is no need to go to such lengths in order to receive the gift of God's presence. One has only to accept it and recognize it as one of the givens of human experience. Like the cloud by day and the pillar of fire by night, God's care is with us always. It is made known in countless ways, but never more clearly than in Jesus Christ to whom Christians are committed as the center of life.

Dietrich Bonhoeffer's *Christ the Center* is a book with powerful impact. Its message that Christ is the center of life comes through clearly. This is nothing new to Christians—or is it? In our theological formulations do we view Christ as being the center? Do we understand and live under this claim, or do we simply ignore it? What about those with whom we share in worship, the persons whose pastors or congregational leaders we are or soon shall be? Is there any real sense of the centrality of Christ who stands among, within, around every relationship?

Bonhoeffer gets at the claim of Christ as center in several ways. He leaves little doubt as to his intention in identifying Christ as *truly* present in the church and *truly* the center of life and history. He is not prepared to attach metaphorical meaning to Christ whom he sees as the real center of human existence. "The meaning of history," says Bonhoeffer, "becomes evident only in the humiliated Christ,"[1] which is his way of referring to the divine logos entering the human logos.

Bonhoeffer argues that the claim about the centrality of Christ is not psychological, but ontological-theological.[2] This is to suggest that the centrality of Christ is both more and other than symbol that points beyond itself. It has its own being, the ontological, which is rooted in and part of God's participation in human history, the theological. This points to far more than Christ's historical influence or someone's vivid memory. What we have in Christ is not the recollection of a bygone era but Christ himself.

The present-historical Christ, in Bonhoeffer's terms, is the same person as the historical Jesus of Nazareth. This is at the heart of Bonhoeffer's Christology. There is, he says, no absolute ground of faith in history. It is only the witness of the Risen One to himself that enables the church to bear witness to him as the Historical One. Jesus Christ is human and thus is present in time and place. Jesus Christ is God and is eternally present everywhere. The two cannot be isolated, because they are not. Christ as center meets us on the firm ground of real life rather than on the spongy soil of imagination.

Why a Christology?

At this point it is fair to clarify the rationale for including a chapter on Christology in a study on stewardship. There is a widespread tendency to prune stewardship well beyond the bare essentials, sometimes even to cut the roots—to fasten onto one or two favorite activities and overlook others. Stewardship is a large concept that must not be artificially limited. Why deal with Christology? Because it is at the very heart of our stewardship. Along with our responsibility for managing resources, we stand with the Apostle Paul "as servants of Christ and stewards of the mysteries of God" (1 Corinthians 4:1).

Persons engaged in the set-apart ministry carry a major role in relating stewardship to the gospel. They are called to preach, but before they can preach with conviction, there must be encounter and commitment. Before they can preach God's love and forgiveness to others, they themselves must have experienced them as realities. Before they can provide helpful training in stewardship, they must see that it starts with a life centered in Christ; and this brings us back to the topic for this chapter.

Returning to Bonhoeffer's thought, he holds that

> ... the proper question to raise in relation to Christ is not one of how or what, but "who are you?" This is the question of faith, and is the only question that can properly be raised since Christ is not shown to be Christ by his works but by his own revelation.... "How are you possible?" is an irrelevant question.... In the Incarnation, once again the question cannot have to do with the how of it. It is only the who? question that will be helpful. The answer ... must be that Christ is the God-man, one person in two natures. This faith that Jesus *is* the Christ, *is* God, cannot be deduced. It is the presupposition of all thought.[3]

As the revelation of God within human history, Jesus Christ is the center of life. This is the faith we hold and by which we try to live. It is where we begin as Christians, so that having made the confession that Jesus is Lord, having accepted the word that

" . . . he who has seen me has seen the Father" (John 14:9), having believed Jesus' claim that "I and the Father are one" (John 10:30), we stand on a faith whose validity we trust. At the very center of that faith is Christ. "The more exclusively we acknowledge and confess Jesus as Lord," says Bonhoeffer, "the more fully the wide range of his dominion will be disclosed to us."[4]

The Meaning of Christ's Centrality

What does it mean for Christ to be central in one's life? Many things, of course but among them, faith in him cannot be taken out and put away according to what might be most convenient. The faith that is centered in Christ is always there for all to see and experience. It is a twenty-four-hour-a-day involvement. This is not to suggest that Christians must be on the nonstop convert-making run from morning till night but that our lives will reflect our faith, whatever the activity of the moment.

One way of finding meaning in the concept of Christ as center is to think of the function performed by an axle in relation to a wheel. The axle gives the wheel its center. It provides something around which the wheel can turn. It keeps the wheel confined, but in that very confinement it brings to the wheel the freedom to be itself and do what it was made to do in a way that could never happen apart from the axle. One has only to picture a runaway wheel, separated from its axle, to be reminded of what life without a proper center is like.

For centuries it was thought—and argued strenuously—that the earth was the center of the universe. We know better now. As earthlings, we are part of the solar system. It is the sun which is at the center. The earth rotates on its axis even as it revolves around the sun. Our atmosphere, the seasons, warmth, photosynthesis, to say nothing of light itself, are all dependent on the sun. At the center of everything for all persons on earth is the sun. Without it, our home would become a dark, lifeless ball of ice.

In something of the same way, Christ is the center of life. Many persons do not acknowledge him as such and look elsewhere for the light. They succeed only in continuing to live in darkness that has already been overcome. It is not so much wrong as tragic, since life that is not centered in God's self-revelation has to be in some respects out of balance. Were it not for Christ, human life itself would lack the center which it has in him through his life, death, and resurrection.

The midpoint of human history was marked by God's coming

in Christ. More than the calendar was divided by that event. We live literally *anno domini,* in the year of our Lord. From the beginning of history until its end, whenever that may come, Christ stands at its center as living witness to God's power and love. Explain it how one will, if one will. In a way not matched by any other, Christ takes his place at the center of life.

The testimony of the scriptures is clear:

> He was in the world, and the world was made through him, yet the world knew him not. He came to his own home, and his own people received him not. But to all who received him, who believed in his name, he gave power to become children of God. . . .
>
> And the Word became flesh and dwelt among us, full of grace and truth; we have beheld his glory; glory as of the only Son from the Father (John 1:10-12, 14).

John by this witness cast his vote for Christ as the center of life, not as an afterthought or an add-on.

The high Christology of Paul's letter to the Colossians comes through especially in the first chapter where Christ is seen as

> . . . the image of the invisible God, the first-born of all creation. . . . He is before all things, and in him all things hold together. He is the head of the body, the church; he is the beginning, the firstborn from the dead, that in everything he might be preeminent. For in him all the fullness of God was pleased to dwell . . . (Colossians 1:15, 17-19).

With Bonhoeffer we could say that such faith comes not by deduction or intellectual analysis, but as with the recognition of Christ as center, it is God's gift to those who believe.

The picture of Christ as the one who holds all things together is not one of frantic seizing, arranging and rearranging, in which everything is disorganized and in a state of turmoil. Quite the opposite, in fact, the picture is one of many members and parts, each doing its assigned task in an orderly and integrated whole. It does not just happen, however, but comes about because of him who is the head, the only one in whom all things can hold together.

The late Robert V. Moss, United Church of Christ (UCC) president, spent a portion of the last weeks of his life working on a paraphrase of the UCC statement of faith:

> In Jesus Christ, the man of Nazareth, our crucified and
> risen Lord, God has come to us and shared our common lot....
> God calls us into the church ... to be servants in the service of
> the whole human family.[5]

In Jesus Christ, God has both come to us and shared common existence, and has tasted the needs, temptations, joys, and sorrows of us common people.

> Jesus, however, did more than share our common needs.
> Jesus *met* the needs of people around him for bread and
> reassurance, healing and wholeness, identity and acceptance,
> friendship and trust, forgiveness and renewal.[6]

To say that Christ is the center of life is to say more than that he occupies a place of honor. It is to point to his involvement with persons where they are. As reported in the gospels his life was spent with and for persons in need: the man lame from birth; the woman with the hemorrhage; Jairus' daughter; Peter's mother-in-law; the woman taken in adultery; the hungry crowds; the tax collectors; Legion, the man who lived among the tombs; the blind man.

Christ was at the center of life in the sense that he offered himself to people where they were. Rather than remaining isolated and aloof, he told the disciples to "let the children come to me, and do not hinder them" (Matthew 19:14). The writer to the Hebrews said: "For we have not a high priest who is unable to sympathize with our weakness, but one who in every respect has been tempted as we are, yet without sinning" (Hebrews 4:15). Christ can be at the center of life because from the beginning, as John says, he has been at the center of all things; and it continues to be so. Again, this is not a matter for proof but for faith.

The evidence seems to suggest that many persons have not yet come to this faith. If Christ is the center of life, he is not the center for them. Perhaps the most important question we can raise is not about others at all, but rather about ourselves. Does what we say we believe about Christ come to life in what we do? Assuming the answer to be both yes and no, should we not be finding ways by which more and more we will be able to answer yes?

Many say, and perhaps rightly so, that Christianity is not a religion of propositions in which salvation is achieved by holding and expressing the right beliefs. This is not to throw beliefs and creeds to the wind, as if they were of little value, but to recognize that they are not of prime importance. Many say also that Christianity is not a religion that grants salvation on the basis of moral excellence and ethical living. These are worthy goals, but neither stands at the top. Christ himself pushed persons to go beyond the requirements of the Law in the practice of their discipleship.

Relationship Makes the Difference

As Christians, we believe it is *relationship* that makes the difference; the relationship initiated by God and made possible in Jesus Christ whom God has placed at the center of life. It is not the church that saves, not even the Bible—as essential as both of these are to the life of faith. It is commitment to the Person that gives us identity as Christians. Recall the baptismal vow to which, though perhaps in different forms, all Christians respond: *Do you believe that Jesus Christ is the Son of God and do you receive him and trust him as your Savior?*

This is what might be called a centering question. It is an invitation to commitment which to some degree is a known quantity. If one can imagine life as a complex and highly diversified business operation, the need for an overall purpose is easy to see. Without it, any part of the business might get carried away with its own importance. Life can become extremely confusing, frustrating, and difficult; but the life that is centered in Christ has what is needed for it to be held together.

That Christ is the center of life is affirmed by many of the world's millions. It has been so for nearly twenty centuries and it will continue to be so as far into the future as human history may go. Much of what is good in society—hospitals, schools, many social agencies—is a legacy from persons who recognized Christ as the center of life.

Our worship includes declarations of faith in Christ, hymns sung to him, prayers offered through him, and sermons preached about him. It is in the Lord's Supper, though, that the celebration of Christ as the center of life touches Christian worshippers most deeply. As we receive the bread and the cup, we take into ourselves the One who in the giving of himself has given life to all, so that, in turn we too may give ourselves and thus *be* Christ for others.

CHAPTER
2

LIFE IS THE CONTEXT
FOR STEWARDSHIP

During a local church study course on stewardship, several sessions included discussions about the implications of stewardship in our daily lives. The group talked about many of the usual topics, as well as some that are frequently overlooked. It spent some time on values and related these to the practice of stewardship. Following a period of silence during which group members confronted themselves about the relationship between earlier discussions and everyday living, one person reported that her view of stewardship had enlarged greatly. With laughter, she recalled for the group her reaction to a phrase the leader had written on the chalk board in the previous session, namely, "the stewardship of facial expression." Her reaction: "Oh no! Not that too!"

Life Is of a Single Piece

That woman was catching a vision of the *whole* of life as the context for stewardship. No longer could she be satisfied to treat stewardship as a concern to be dealt with only at church. For her it was becoming a major ingredient of life in all its aspects. This is one of the most basic truths about stewardship—that ordinary, everyday life is where it happens.

Perhaps in no other connection can the fact that life is of a single piece be seen more clearly. Distinctions between sacred and secular disappear when one understands that life, whatever it may involve, is the setting within which persons act out their stewardship. This is to say that all of life is a sacred trust over which we exercise some kind of care. It is to avoid the trap of dualism which would make some parts of life subject to stewardship and leave others exempt from it. Traditionally, the church has been too much concerned about the 10 percent and too little about the 90 percent.

The Genesis accounts of creation leave no uncertainty about the role of man and woman. They were to be the resident managers. They were to till and keep the garden. They were to people the earth and subdue it, to have dominion over it, to look after the interests of the Creator and to oversee every good thing that had been made. Their stewardship, far from being segregated from life, was bound up inextricably with it. It was in the plowing of the soil and the planting of the seed, in the gathering of the fruit and the tending of the flocks and herds, that the highest of God's creation lived up to their calling.

George S. Siudy, Jr. writes of human cocreation as a corollary of belief in creation.

> The calling of Israel, says Bible scholar Hans-Reudi Weber, included not only what God had given, "but also collaboration with God in developing the riches of this earth, in transforming the world and bringing it to its glorious consummation."
>
> ... In this covenant of cocreativity our institutions as well as our material goods are resources. Not only money, but agencies whose objectives include work for justice, peace and human wholeness and faith itself are instruments for use in cocreation with the divine.[1]

In keeping with God's calling of Israel and of all humanity, the whole of life must be seen as the context for stewardship.

Rather than a collaboration with God in development, one gets the impression that much of what is going on in life today cannot be described as other than the exploiting of what is here for the self-interest of the few, rather than for the well-being of the many. It stands as a denial of the human family's right to adequate food, clean water, pure air, and freedom from disease. Between college terms our son was employed at a large plastics factory. He complained on occasion about the irritants to breathing picked up from the ever-present airborne dust. In a newspaper article the president of the company was reported as having spoken out against stringent governmental regulations on carcinogen levels for plastics factories since these would "... cause economic hardship to the multi-billion dollar plastics industry."[2] The plastics industry, unfortunately, is not alone in this. One has only to think of the coal mines, the diamond mines, the asbestos and insulation factories. What can be said of factory owners who fail to value employee well-being and health sufficiently to provide adequate safeguards?

The Holistic View

If life is the context for stewardship and if human life is at least a major portion of that life, it follows that the stewardship of human life cannot be treated lightly. If we are cocreators with God in the development of the earth—and even if we are not, but are just tenders of the garden—how much greater must be our responsibility for one another than for the atmosphere, the animals and plants, the soil, the rivers, lakes, and seas.

If life is the context for stewardship, what about the care of ourselves? What about the eating of proper food and not too much of it, the drinking of healthful beverages, being sure to have adequate rest on a regular basis and refusing to take pride in addiction to work—"I work seventy-five hours a week"; "I never take a day off"; "I haven't had a vacation in ten years"? Are not all of these involved? What about learning to play and find joy in recreation? What of opening oneself to new ideas and other persons? All of these have to do with the stewardship of self.

It is the holistic view of life as a trust from God that one finds in the Bible. It is the same holistic view that is set forth so movingly in the film, *How Good Life Can Be.*[3] The film presents vignettes of persons who take seriously but with joy life as the context for stewardship. A man describes the simple experience of freeing a stranger's icebound car. A woman shares the happiness she receives from teaching handicapped youngsters to swim. In another segment an older man helps little children plant trees. In still another, the focus is on a man who plays the piano for a senior citizens' hot lunch program sponsored by his church. Not one of these is a particularly religious activity, but every one of them is a part of life and therefore fully within the context of stewardship.

One of the temptations to which church people often succumb is the dividing up of life into bins or compartments that are effectively separated from one another. What takes place during the service of worship and much of what happens within the church building is kept in one bin. What happens in the workaday world is kept in another, perhaps not even by design. "Business is business" though, and "one has to get ahead." So the life bin is kept well separated from stewardship.

Brother Lawrence, the self-described " . . . great awkward fellow who broke everything"[4] and became a monk in the barefoot Carmelite order at Paris, by his practice of the presence of God came to understand life as the context for his own stewardship. He had no separate bins.

> . . . In the greatest hurry of business in the kitchen he still preserved his recollection and heavenly-mindedness. He was never hasty nor loitering, but did each thing in its season, with an even, uninterrupted composure and tranquillity of spirit. "The time of business," said he, "does not with me differ from the time of prayers, and in the noise and clatter of my kitchen, while several persons are at the same time calling for different things, I possess God in as great tranquillity as if I were upon my knees at the blessed sacrament."[5]

Scriptural Studies

In writing to the Corinthians about the generous giving of the Christians in Macedonia, Paul says that they gave not only according to their means, but beyond their means and of their own free will. Their giving was a response to need, but it was much more than that. It was a result of their already having made a gift that could not be measured in money. "First," declares Paul, "they gave *themselves* to the Lord and to us by the will of God" (2 Corinthians 8:5). That is to say, they recognized the relationship of all of life—and of their very selves—to stewardship.

The Greek construction of this passage is instructive. Quite literally it reads: "and not as we hoped toward [or expected] but themselves they gave first to the Lord . . . " Note the order of the words and the consequent emphasis: *themselves they gave first to the Lord.* Therein lies the explanation for their eager sharing of money. It was preceded by a far more valuable gift. The Macedonians were not involved in a mere fund-raising appeal. There was no need to talk them into something. Their giving had gone beyond money even before the first gifts were gathered.

Perhaps in the entire New Testament there is no passage that comes down harder on the need for seeing life as the context for stewardship than the Matthew 25:31-46 account of the Last Judgment. The scene is the gathering of all the nations before the Son of Man who separates them as a shepherd separates sheep from goats. The test for being on the king's right hand is very simple: the giving of food, drink, clothing, welcome to the stranger, and visits to the prisoner. It does not matter that those who gave did not recognize the Lord in those to whom they went. It would have made little difference, for already they were doing what needed to be done and would have continued to do so. The context for their stewardship was the life of which they were a part and in which they chose to respond.

On the other hand, one has the feeling that those who withheld their gifts would gladly have given them if only someone had listed them as requirements; if only someone had told *them* that the persons in need were the Lord. Theirs apparently was a calculating style. They would have changed their ways had they known it would make a difference in their own welfare. Of course they would have been more careful of the needs of others if there had been the slightest hint that it would show up on the permanent record. The point is that life as we know it is where we meet the One to whom we owe our final stewardship.

The prophet Micah opened up the same truth for people of his day who thought they could satisfy the demands of Yahweh by appearing occasionally at public worship with yearling calves to be given as burnt offerings. No, it was not thousands of rams or ten thousands of rivers of precious olive oil, certainly not a human sacrifice that would atone for sin. All of these missed the mark badly. Micah's conclusion: "He has showed you, O man, what is good; and what does the Lord require of you but to do justice, and to love kindness, and to walk humbly with your God?" (Micah 6:8).

Stewardship in the Midst of Life

It is in the midst of life, not apart from it, that we are called to stewardship: in the madcap cities of today, amid the roar of supersaver jet travel instead of the clip-clop pace of horse and buggy days that linger as a fading memory; in the communities of today that serve as little more than temporary stopping-off places between moves, not in the stable towns of another age where families lived for generations. Whatever we may think of life in our world, it is the only context we have for our stewardship.

Just what is this life? It is time, talent, financial resources. Without *time* there is no life. What we do with the time we all have in equal amounts varies greatly. Some people while the hours away, not doing much of anything. Some never have enough time to do all they want. Some dread every new day and can hardly endure another night. Some use time as an irreplaceable gift: they write books; they build houses; they visit with friends; they go to movies; they sleep; they think; they practice; they study; they play; they work; they help others.

Time might be described as the quantitative measure of life. It may be thought of as minutes, half-days, eight-hour work periods, twenty-four-hour days, weeks, months, years, decades, centuries. Here it is, ready to be used as we will. It is neither good nor bad nor in between. Time *is*, and it is at our disposal. It is one way of describing life as the context for stewardship.

Here, the doctrine of freedom is illustrated and documented. What one does with time likely will reflect other choices. While the process of determining those choices is complicated and influenced by choices that others make, it is one over which we maintain control. There are days when we might prefer to use time differently but still choose to do what we do not prefer at the moment in order to accomplish some longer-term goal or complete some task. Time is among God's many gifts. Within it we live out our stewardship.

Talent is another way of talking about life. This is an area of vast differences and apparent inequities. A young woman in a weekend workshop shared her feeling that she was totally lacking in any talent which she could identify. Something happened to her during those few days, however, and she came to see the gifts that were hers. With that discovery came a transformation within her that served to enhance and multiply the talents she already possessed.

During another gift-naming exercise, a church leader sat in the center of a circle formed by a small group of colleagues, each of whom in turn placed his or her hand on the person and spoke to him of gifts that he possesses. Besides being moved deeply by that experience and affirmed by it, he was also brought to a new awareness of some gifts that had come to be taken for granted. Stewardship is expressed through the particular talents and gifts that a person has. What one does with those gifts, how one develops them, whether one shares them with others, is up to that person. One's stewardship is probably revealed more fully by what is done with what one has than by the mere having of gifts, even though they are many.

Financial resources provide another opportunity for stewardship and an index of it. In our money economy they are a significant expression of life. Money has been described as stored energy. It functions as the primary medium of exchange, but it is more. It stands as a symbol of time and talent, even of life itself. In a real sense, one trades all of these for money so as to be able to secure desired goods or services. What one does in that trading process is itself a part of stewardship. How one goes about earning money says as much about that person's stewardship as does the way in which the money is used.

From time to time, studies are published showing the spending patterns of persons in this country for items in, for example, twelve large categories. Certain values are reflected in those expenditures and in all the expenditures people make. One task of the Christian is to see money as a part of life and therefore as a part of overall stewardship. While one ought not infer too much from studies such as the one noted above, questions arise when expenditures for all religious and welfare activities are less than half the amount spent on alcoholic beverages and only one-fifth of the amount spent on recreation.[6] The shocking comparison is with United States military expenditures which consistently are many times more than the amount spent on religion and welfare: $144.2 billion in fiscal 1976[7] as opposed to $13.8 billion.

When one thinks of money and stewardship, it is essential to think in terms of the total resources at a person's disposal. Given the various commitments, responsibilities, and needs that are represented in a person, how are these brought into a balance that makes sense? The stewardship of money extends far beyond the question of how much shall be given away. It includes as well that which is kept and spent and invested.

A parishioner once observed to the writer that life would be much simpler if everything were clear-cut. Life is not always so sharply defined, however; indeed, frequently it is not, and part of the excitement of living is engaging in the struggle to find one's way when the issues are clouded. By the same token, things would be a lot easier if stewardship were a bit more restricted; if it were confined, say, to a single area or to no more than a few. There is no way, though, that it can be hemmed in, for life—all of it—is the context for stewardship.

CHAPTER
3

STEWARDSHIP IS THE PRACTICE OF FAITH

One of the foundation stones for the stewardship concept set forth in this study is to be found in creationist theology which takes as its point of departure the belief that God always is at the heart of creation. The world did not appear as the result of some cosmic accident, nor did it put itself together. All that *is,* and we are only beginning to discover what that includes, came to be in response to the creative word of God. The ancient storytellers and the writers of scripture were infinitely more concerned with the roots of humankind than with the process of how the seed was developed. They started with the most basic assumption of all: "In the beginning . . . " (Genesis 1:1).

The Initiative Is With God
The initiative is always with God. It was so in creation, and it was so in the covenant with Abram to whom God said: "I will make of you a great nation, and I will bless you, and make your name great, so that you will be a blessing" (Genesis 12:2). It was God who took the initiative with Moses at the burning bush, in the deliverance from Egypt, and on Mount Sinai. It was Yahweh whom Isaiah saw high and lifted up, to whom he responded, "Here I am! Send me" (Isaiah 6:8). It was God who " . . . was in Christ reconciling the world to himself" (2 Corinthians 5:19).

In relation to stewardship, God is the builder of the house—

the world—in which God's children live. God is also the builder of the spiritual house—the congregation—in which all members take their places as living stones, with Christ as the chief cornerstone. The root word for stewardship in the New Testament is *oikos*. It is a word whose background and meanings can add greatly to one's understanding of stewardship. We turn now to Brattgard for help in this regard.

> Besides its original meaning, "place of residence," it also suggests, not least of all, the fellowship which unites those who belong to the same household, first the family, but this could include the relations as well. Greek and Hebrew have no word for "family;" they use the term *oikos* or *beth* respectively. . . . *Oikos*, therefore, implies domestic fellowship, or, in the broader sense, the family, including the sons, the servants, and the families of guests. . . . The decisive thing here is not the blood relationship, but participation in the same fortunes, the same work, the same success and failure, and the same dangers. . . . Another decisive meaning attached to the term *oikos*, met in certain biblical texts, is this, that it is God who builds this "house." . . .
>
> Over and above this general meaning of the concept "house," however, *oikos* possesses a more unique meaning when it is used in the combination "God's house," *oikos tou theou*. . . .
>
> . . . From its basic connotation of "place of residence," the meaning of the term has been deepened to designate the Christian congregation with the spiritual life which exists there. . . . To be God's *oikonomos* [steward] and have insight into his *oikonomia* [stewardship] are organically related to life in the congregation.[1]

The Management Is Ours

Brattgard goes on to point out that the image presented in the New Testament of the first Christian congregations as God's *oikos*, made up of separate houses or families, is essential if one is to grasp the stewardship idea. To be a steward in the biblical sense assumes the ability to manage one's own house. "Any participation in the work of the congregation, effective as it may be, which leads to the neglect of our own house and its care can never be in agreement with the biblical understanding of stewardship."[2]

The Greek word for steward, *oikonomos*, was used widely long before the Christian era. John Reumann gives a number of examples of the term's use in pre-Christian writings going back as early as about 300 B.C.[3] He notes that this term which has come to hold rich meaning for Christians is one that was in the air during the first century. Christians simply appropriated a word that had been in common usage in politics and applied it to themselves. Reumann suggests that *oikonomos* in its earlier usages was similar to our words "comptroller" and "secretary" as the latter is used in political and governmental terminology and to some extent in the church (e.g., general secretary).

The related word for stewardship, *oikonomia*, has a similarly long history, as pointed out by Brattgard:

> In the main, one can speak of four different primary meanings attached to the word through the years. Originally the term referred to the management, direction, or administration of a household with its variety of concerns. But this meaning soon broadened, so that the term came to refer to the administration of an entire state, particularly in the military and economic areas. The next step, to a more general meaning, was not far ahead. The word group thus came, by degrees, to denote assumption of a whole variety of tasks [in the fields of medicine, the arts, literature, logic]. . . . By degrees it came to denote the administration of the universe, and it was quite natural, therefore, that it came to have religious significance.[4]

In the New Testament the word *oikonomia* appears rather infrequently. When it does appear, it is possible to detect three fundamental meanings.

> In the first place, this word refers to the task of the steward as such, and also to stewardship itself. . . . [Secondly,] Paul uses the term in connection with his apostolic office, and . . . looks upon this task as a trust.[5]

This can be seen readily in 1 Corinthians 4:1 where Paul says, "This is how one should regard us, as servants of Christ and stewards *[oikonomoi]* of the mysteries of God." The third meaning of *oikonomia* described by Brattgard is evident in the prison epistles where it refers to " . . . God's all-encompassing plan of salvation, in which Christ stands at the center."[6]

Perhaps this is enough to establish the richness of the biblical view of stewardship which is much broader than that held by many Christians. Those who would limit stewardship to the gathering of money reflect a grossly inaccurate and uninformed understanding. Much more than money is involved in stewardship. This was the burden of Chapter 2 in which the case was made that nothing short of life itself will suffice for the practice of a proper stewardship, as interpreted in the New Testament.

Stewardship and Faith Belong Together

It follows, then, that stewardship must not, indeed cannot, be limited to the practice of religion. That is, the responsibilities of stewardship cannot be discharged by making a financial commitment to the church, as desirable as that is, or by making extra gifts when the need arises. Those responsibilities cannot be fulfilled even with the decision to tithe. It is the whole of life over which we exercise our stewardship, which is to say that stewardship is the practice of faith.

Faith has much more to do with relationships—with oneself, with other persons, with the whole created order, and with God—than with beliefs of the head. The crucial question about one's faith is: What difference does it make, or how does it affect one's life? This is not to denigrate the importance of clear thinking and carefully considered beliefs. It is, rather, to hold that something else comes before them.

All persons of faith are themselves practicing theologians. Their theology may not be evident to them. It probably has not been thought out, much less articulated. This, however, does not make it any less real, for it is operative in their lives. The key word in the *Acts of the Apostles* is *Acts*. It is a translation of the Greek *praxeis* which could just as well be rendered *doings*. This New Testament book is a rich commentary on the theology of the early church. The theology appears in the simple reporting of what those apostles did, not in a systematic presentation of beliefs.

At the beginning of this chapter, reference was made to creationist theology as one of the foundation stones for stewardship. Another of those stones is incarnational theology, which begins with God's coming in Christ, but goes on to the idea that all Christians are little Christs to one another and to their neighbors. It is not pressing incarnational theology unduly to say that stewardship is the incarnation, the bringing to life, of one's beliefs. In the practicing of our faith, our word becomes flesh.

It is possible, of course, that we reveal more about ourselves than we intend as we practice our own faith and live out our stewardship. Might it even be that there is considerable self-disclosure in what we choose not to share with others? The rather general secrecy attached to financial affairs—earnings, obligations, investments, giving—may say a great deal about our own anxieties and about our own stewardship.

One has to wonder what the record would say to future generations if the *doings* or *acts* of the one who writes or those who read these words were reported. Would such a report reflect a faith in Christ that is evident in all of life? Would it have the effect of inspiring such faith in others, or would it be a discouragement to them? All of us are theologians at the practical level. Whatever we may say, what we *do* is the reliable indicator of what we really believe.

By the very nature of human existence, stewardship is built into the order of things. There is no question as to whether persons shall be stewards. The only question is what kind of stewards will they be? Will they, for example, be like the dishonest steward who took advantage of his master (Luke 16:1-9), the rich fool who believed in full-barn salvation (Luke 12:15-21), the one-talent servant who dug in the ground and hid his master's money (Matthew 25:14-30)?

By the very nature of Christian experience, stewardship is the practice of faith. Persons who embrace the faith find in their service to Christ the perfect freedom which for others exists only as an unrealized dream. They do not fight stewardship since it is a vital part of their faith, nor do they keep their faith under cover, since they have chosen to *live* by faith. Stewardship, therefore, is not a requirement imposed from the outside, but the normal way by which persons of faith witness to that faith and express their own commitment.

Faithfulness, Wisdom, Accountability

What does it mean when we say that stewardship is the practice of faith? Without getting lost in detail, we can observe that " . . . the basic characteristics of a true steward are . . . faithfulness and wisdom, plus a concentration on the day of reckoning."[7] This is made clear in the Luke 12:42-48 passage:

> And the Lord said, "Who then is the faithful and wise steward, whom his master will set over his household, to give them their portion of food at the proper time? Blessed is that servant whom his master when he comes will find so doing. Truly I tell you, he will set him over all his possessions. But if that servant says to himself, 'My master is delayed in coming,' and begins to beat the menservants and maidservants, and to eat and drink and get drunk, the master of that servant will come on a day when he does not expect him and at an hour he

does not know, and will punish him, and put him with the un-faithful. And that servant who know his master's will, but did not make ready or act according to his will, shall receive a severe beating. But he who did not know, and did what deserved a beating, shall receive a light beating. Everyone to whom much is given, of him will much be required; and of him to whom men commit much they will demand the more."

Faithfulness thus can be identified as a chief characteristic of the good steward.

Faithfulness implies the possibility of unfaithfulness. The freedom we have to choose is a strong sign of God's confidence in us. God offers us the opportunity to use, manage, and develop the resources and gifts placed in our care, all of which belong ultimately to God. Faith is denied and confidence is betrayed if faithfulness is lacking, so that both God's risk and our responsibility are great.

Along with faithfulness, wisdom is a mark of good stewardship. In the passage quoted above, the steward was not given detailed instructions. Indeed, there was only one order: to supply the members of the household with "their portion of food at the proper time" (Luke 12:42). This allowed for considerable latitude and left a great deal to the steward's own judgment. What was the portion to be given to the several persons in the household? What was the proper time? These were left to the steward. Except for the single guideline, everything was to be determined by the steward who apparently was expected to act independently of the master but to do so with wisdom.

The anxious steward of Matthew 25:18 was more fearful than wise. He buried his money and took comfort in having safeguarded the one talent which the master had entrusted to him. His need for security prevented his responding with imaginative wisdom. The best he could do was dig a hole, bury the money, and congratulate himself on coming up with such a fail-safe plan. "In such a life, which thinks itself free of risk, the great risk is this, that one will lose 'what he has.' "[8]

If wisdom and faithfulness are essential to the biblical view of stewardship, so also is accountability. This is to recognize that what the steward has belongs to another. The *oikonomos* is responsible directly and exclusively to the Lord. Accounting does not have to do with what one thought, planned, or hoped to do, but only with what, in fact, was done. The questions to be answered by such accounting are: Was the steward faithful, and did the steward act in wisdom? These are questions for us to ask ourselves.

Another writer puts the issue clearly when he says:

> Any slave can follow a work-sheet or check-list, but a steward works from the knowledge of his master and what his master's interests and purposes are. He knows that he will be called to give an accounting of his stewardship in due time. But he is left to determine for himself what is the appropriate and responsible thing to do in handling his master's business. . . . This rules out all simple legalism or moralisms when it comes to exercising his vocation. The steward has to be as wise as he is faithful.[9]

It comes back, then, to the relationship between steward and master; a relationship in which the practice of faith cannot be missing. Fisher says that "Christian stewardship and the gospel are inseparable. It roots essentially not in programs but in a dynamic relationship with the living God."[10]

For the Christian, faith is life; it has to be or it is counterfeit. The claims that one makes about religious beliefs stand or fall when they are measured by the harsh reality of life. Stewardship, therefore if it is understood as a condition of human existence, must involve the practice of faith. It cannot offer the luxury of stopping with words. As the writer of James says,

> What does it profit, my brethren, if a man says he has faith but has not works? Can his faith save him? If a brother or sister is ill-clad and in lack of daily food, and one of you says to them, "Go in peace, be warmed and filled," without giving them the things needed for the body, what does it profit? So faith by itself, if it has no works, is dead (James 2:14-17).

The practice of stewardship is the calling of every person, although some seem not to know, or if they know, seem not to care. By their own public confession of faith, however, Christians not only care about the call to stewardship, but commit themselves to live within it. This calling applies to every part of life, so that nothing can be removed from its influence. Stewardship is a trust given us by God. It can be misused and betrayed, or it can reflect the faith of persons whose lives are centered in Christ.

CHAPTER
4

FAITH IS GOD'S GIFT
TO THE CHURCH

The importance of faith to the life of the individual Christian hardly needs to be argued. Clarity, however, is often lacking in what is meant by faith. It has already been pointed out in these pages that the primary meaning of faith is relational rather then intellectual. Indeed, faith that relies on propositions cannot be faith in the biblical sense. One's beliefs are formed in the presence of significant faith relationships. "The attitude which sees the whole of life as a sacred trust," observes one writer, is " . . . a response of the whole person to the divine activity as it is encountered in the person himself, in the Christian community, and in the world."[1]

The same writer goes on to make his case:

For Christian faith the central reality of life is the grace of God. Man receives his existence as a gift. At every point in his life he is dependent on resources and activities which he does not create but which are freely made available to him. Ultimately he is more a receiver that a doer. Yet his very status as a recipient calls on him to use his gifts in responsibility to the Giver and to other recipients. He is, as it were, addressed and summoned to give an answer by one who confronts him and on whom he finally depends. The starting point and continuing source of Christian faith and life, and hence of stewardship, is thus man's experience of and faithful response to the manifold grace of God, to whom he owes all.

. . . Christian faith arises initially as a joyous, grateful response to the creative and redemptive action of God which is decisively focused in Jesus Christ.[2]

To say that faith is God's gift to the church is to say that it is the relationship that counts. The relationship is close and warm, much like that of parent and child, and it is dependent only on God's making it possible and our responding. If we are living in a right relationship with God, we will use and enjoy the gifts that come to us, but we will never place those gifts above the Giver. Brattgard puts it well:

Man trusts in God himself, and not in his gifts . . . Only in such a spirit can we relinquish his gifts without despair, should they be taken from us . . . If we despair when these things are taken away, it is clear that our trust was in them and not in God.[3]

The argument can be carried further. The only proper relationship with God is the unconditional one, the one in which persons worship God in faith and receive God's gifts in gratitude, whether few or many, large or small, ordinary or outstanding.

The gifts entrusted to us are now looked upon first of all as something to administer, something which we ourselves cannot have at our disposal. In gratitude we return these to the Giver—by using them in the service of our neighbor.[4]

If, as we have said, faith is described by relationship, then it seems clear that the biblical idea of stewardship has much to do with faith since it has to do with all of life. God is the one who calls us into being and reaches out to us in love. From God's side, the relationship is already established in the same way that our salvation is already accomplished. In both instances, the only uncertain element is our response. If we remain faithless, we become selfish and enslaved by things. When, on the other hand, we accept our role as stewards, the life of faith is begun.

Faith is a word that has different meanings. There are places in the New Testament where it refers to little more than the Christian religion, but in the large majority of cases where the word is used, the meaning goes back to the Hebrew concept as identified by the words:

. . . firmness, reliability, or steadfastness. To believe is to hold on to something firmly with conviction and confidence . . . Usually it is a person, rather than a statement, which is believed; and in the context of men's relation to God the verb always implies personal conviction and trust arising within direct personal relationship. The NT Greek reflects this point by introducing a preposition ('believe *in* . . . ') in almost every instance where more is intended than mere credence.

If then a person 'holds sure in God', he may be said to 'have faith.'[5]

The stance of Christians generally is that God not only acts first but makes it possible for persons to live as loyal servants in the faith relationship. What is found in persons of faith, therefore, is not something of their own doing. It is God who makes the believer firm and trustworthy. The believer's part is to lay hold of God's promised acts by which one is sustained and recreated.

Illustrations of Faith

An illustration of this comes to mind from a recent experience. Upon landing at a small airport, we had occasion to watch a barnstorming pilot and his courageous, if foolhardy, female assistant prepare for some stunt flying that included what is known in the business as wing walking. The young woman climbed to the upper wing of the biplane, was strapped in at the waist and shoulders, had guy wires to hang onto, and stood against an upright brace. The moment of truth arrived when the pilot got into the open cockpit, started the engine, and taxied to the end of the runway in preparation for takeoff. Within a few minutes the plane, with the woman standing on the wing, came roaring down the runway and into the air.

The small group of onlookers thought the show was over and most of them left. The few who remained, however, realized that the show was just beginning. Off in the distance they were able to see the plane as it was maneuvered through a series of inside loops and barrel rolls. It was difficult to tell whether the wing walker was still in position until the plane returned to the airport and made its approach. She was standing as the plane touched down, and there was relief among the watchers when they saw that she had survived. Conversation with the young woman and the pilot revealed that this was her second time on the wing but her first time for any maneuvers.

In this experience is demonstrated the difference between

faith and more casual belief. The pilot, according to airport personnel, is widely known for his skill. He is an accomplished stunt flyer who makes appearances all across the country. His reputation in flying circles is something to envy. Most people, upon learning the facts about him and seeing his name in large letters on the fuselage, would not doubt that he could fly with someone standing on the wing; indeed, they would believe it readily.

Without question, the young woman who allowed herself to be talked into wing walking, with all the obvious risks and dangers, must have believed that Wayne Pierce is a super pilot. Thus far, we are talking about intellectual belief. When the woman actually stood on the wing, however, and felt the plane rolling on the runway, first slowly, then faster and faster until it was airborne, *that* was something else. It was a kind of faith, at least. For whatever reasons and out of whatever backgrounds, there was a relationship of trust between the person with the wind in her face and the man at the controls. The faith may not have been recognized for what it was, but it was acted upon and lived out.

I remember one of my theology teachers making the case that virtually everyone operates at some level of faith. One example cited was that of driving a car on a highway at fifty miles an hour in the face of oncoming traffic going at about the same speed hardly more than three feet away. Most drivers believe that most other drivers are careful and will stay in their own lane. Consequently, they exercise faith by acting on that belief and by driving on two-lane roads with minimal anxiety. We need not linger over the fact that such faith is sometimes misplaced, as evidenced by the head-on collisions and other accidents that are all too common.

For Christians who experience God as the giver of all that is good, including the faith that enables them to trust God even in the presence of the most adverse circumstances, life can be lived in the peace that goes beyond understanding. Think of those who have suffered in various ways. Very often they have risen far above their sufferings, so that their illness, injury, handicap, deprivation, or grief have served not to undo their faith but to reinforce it. Their faith was not a human achievement for which they should be praised but a gift from God to whom thanksgiving should be offered.

A stewardship executive, in the course of a field visit, fell from a porch deck and was immediatlely paralyzed from the chest down. There was little hope, if any, for recovery. Paralysis, it seemed, would be permanent. Subsequent examinations and developments confirmed that prognosis. Such a Job-like happening might well be the occasion for a person to curse God and, for all practical purposes, die. This friend, however, has not found it so. He is grateful to be alive and, in the spirit of a good steward, is determined to do what he can with what he has. God has extended to him the gift of faith and he rejoices in it.

Even as these words are written another friend lies at what must be the opening door of death. In his hospital room he is numbed by medication to ease his pain; too weak to raise a hand. Fully aware of his approaching death, he holds fast to his own faith and is supported in that faith by the presence of caring persons. Through them God draws him close to the divine presence and brings the gift of a shared faith that grows deeper even at the ebb tide of life.

There is a former parishioner who comes to mind. Mildred called one evening, weeping, to ask if the pastor would come over right away since she was afraid that her husband, Louis, had died. Upon arriving, it was apparent that her fears were well founded. The emergency crew left and the doctor arrived, only to be followed by the funeral director. Louis had been sitting at the dining room table and without a word had fallen from his chair to the floor, instantly dead. In the days following, Mildred said to the writer, "I don't know what I would do without my faith." She was an active member of the church and her faith was a gift of God to her through the household of faith.

The importance of the church in God's gift of faith to each person can be seen as one examines the development of a newborn baby. Apart from other persons, there is no way that a baby would be able to be a person. Baum says:

> We are able to speak because others have spoken to us. We achieve a certain self-awareness and are able to put something of what we are into words because we participate in the language of mother, father, the family, and the wider community. Without the language to which we are introduced, we would not have a mental life. One may even go further and suggest that a man does not achieve consciousness at all unless there was someone who summoned him when he was a baby.[6]

The Church and Faith

In much the same way, the community of faith becomes the channel for God's gift of faith to individuals. It also provides a framework within which one's response to God may be given, tested, revised, and constantly developed. Following Baum's logic, apart from the community of faith, one could have no hope of becoming a person of faith. The gift, therefore, is not distributed to persons in isolation. Just as a baby cannot come to be truly a person except in the presence of others, so can a person come to meaningful and enduring faith only within the community.

Even for the church, though, faith is not arrived at by anything the body of followers may do. The writer of Ephesians says it well: "For by grace you have been saved through faith; and this is not your own doing, it is the gift of God—not because of works, lest any man should boast" (Ephesians 2:8-9). Similarly, Paul writes that " . . . they are justified by his grace as a gift, through the redemption which is in Christ Jesus" (Romans 3:24).

How is God's gift of faith given to the church? Surely it is not only through the act of quietistic meditation after the fashion of the mystics, as helpful as that discipline may be. Most certainly, the gift is given in part through worship and preaching, through great music and the singing of hymns, through the scriptures, and through the gathered community. Let it be said plainly, though, that God's gift of faith comes first and most completely in Christ, the center of life and the source of faith. This is only to remind ourselves of what we already know, namely, that in the words of Paul once again, " . . . God was in Christ reconciling the world to himself" (2 Corinthians 5:19).

The Promises of God

The promises of God can be gathered up in the parables and other teachings of Jesus. They can be pointed to by words such as *love* and *forgiveness:*

> But while he was yet at a distance, his father saw him and had compassion, and ran and embraced him and kissed him. . . . But the father said to his servants, . . . "let us eat and make merry; for this my son was dead, and is alive again" (Luke 15:30, 22a, 24a).

God's promises are also pointed to by the call to *wholeness:* "Jesus said to him, 'Rise, take up your pallet and walk.' And at once the man was healed, and he took up his pallet and walked" (John 5:8-9); and by the assurance that *God cares:*

> "Lord, if you had been here, my brother would not have died."

> When Jesus saw her weeping, and the Jews who came with her also weeping, he was deeply moved in spirit and troubled. . . . Jesus wept (John 11:32b, 33, 35).

One writer has said: "God keeps his promises, and Jesus Christ is the guarantee that it is so!"[7] If we believe that it was the promise of God which Jesus spoke when he said, "I will not leave you desolate" (John 14:18), we can also believe that God grants the gift of faith to the church which itself stands as fulfillment of the promise. Through his own body, the church, Christ ministers in love to all who will receive the gift of himself. It must be seen here, and will be developed in the next chapter, that the church is not the stopping point but serves rather as a continuing means of God's grace.

All who have been recipients of God's gift of faith could witness to the gift's being mediated and nurtured within the community of believers. One can think of particular persons and events within whom and through which the gift of faith was extended. Without consciously dwelling on it, perhaps, many persons are themselves powered by, and witnesses to, the kind of faith that causes others to want to share it. They are persons in our churches, very ordinary and still in need of considerable polishing, but transmitters of the gift of faith which God would give to all.

Returning to an earlier theme, we may summarize by saying that since stewardship assumes faithfulness, wisdom, and accountability in all things and since faith has to do with all of life's relationships, stewardship and faith are very close together indeed. Fisher is on the mark when he says that "stewardship is every Christian's true vocation."[8] That is what the life of faith is all about: to live in God's house and to take our places as responsible living stones in the walls of that house.

CHAPTER
5

THE CHURCH IS GOD'S PARTNER IN MISSION

Some persons speak of *God's house* and understand by that term the building in which a congregation gathers for worship and study. We have seen, however, that God's house in the biblical sense has much more to do with the body of believers and their life together than with a building, whether simple meeting house or gothic structure. "The church," says Brunner, "is not 'something', neither a building nor a form of polity, neither an organization nor a institution; the church is nothing but persons, namely, human persons who are joined together through the person of their Heavenly Lord."[1] In the same vein, another scholar points out that " 'Church' in [the New Testament] translates Gk. *ecclesia*, which always means an assembly of people, and cannot mean a building."[2]

The Church as Christ's Body

It was against the backdrop of such a dynamic view of the church that the Apostle Paul painted his image-packed picture for the Christians at Corinth:

> For just as the body is one and has many members, and all the members of the body, though many, are one body, so it is with Christ. For by one Spirit we were all baptized into one body—Jews or Greeks, slaves or free—and all were made to drink of one Spirit (1 Corinthians 12:12-13).

In Paul's understanding, the body serves as an analogy but as much more than that since the church *is* the real, living body of Christ.

Paul continues: "For the body does not consist of one member but of many" (1 Corinthians 12:14). The body is an unbelievably complex organism whose parts are deeply and, in some cases, mysteriously interrelated. Each member is important but none can substitute for the whole body of which it is only a part. How absurd to suppose that a gigantic eye, a six foot nose, or a one-hundred-fifty pound ear could be the body! "If the foot should say, 'Because I am not a hand, I do not belong to the body,' that would not make it any less a part of the body" (1 Corinthians 12:15). Here Paul's imagination comes to the fore and he has a foot making a sad-sack speech, the essence of which is that "I don't belong since I am what I am." Who cares that a foot cannot speak? It represents accurately the feelings of some of the Corinthians who thought that unless one were an ecstatic speaker he or she could not really be a part of the church.

The Apostle brings his argument to conclusion when he says: "Now you are the body of Christ and individually members of it" (1 Corinthians 12:27). It is both the individual member's importance and the relationship of each to the whole which he holds up. Paul does not say to the Christians at Corinth that they are *like* the body of Christ in their community of faith, but that " ... you *are* the body of Christ ... " Theologically, this is a statement about the Incarnation. It says a great deal about the relationship of the church to the Christ of faith. It indicates also a high view of the church, though not in the liturgical sense often associated with that phrase.

What persons bring to the church by way of their individual gifts ought not be minimized, but neither should there be any doubt that it is the individual member's integration into the whole body of Christ that brings life and meaning. At this point we turn again to one of Brunner's sermons:

> "The individual Christian" is really a misunderstanding; there is no such thing. Just as there cannot be an individual hand or an individual arm—it is then cut off and dead—so there cannot be an individual Christian. A Christian is always a member of the community or he is no Christian.[3]

The body that is working properly is a delight. The hand and eye coordination required in many activities is an illustration. In contrast, the body that is fighting with itself has difficulty. For example, a person who suffers from cerebral palsy or multiple sclerosis or cancer does not enjoy the blessings of bodily unity that many of us take for granted. It cannot be so with those who belong to Christ's body.

It is Christ who is the unifying force in the church. In him, individuals come into true community. They give up their natural inclination toward independence and find their places as members of his body. This is radically different from the paper membership which is all too common in many churches. It is participation in the church, not just a *record* of one's having been received, that confirms membership. It is the *practice* of our faith in company with others that identifies us as members of Christ's living body.

This faith, though developed and nurtured in the community of believers, is not an in-house activity. There is nothing esoteric about it, nothing hidden, nothing which requires exclusivity. It could not be so since " . . . God so loved the *world* that he gave his only son . . . For God sent the Son into the world, not to condemn the world, but that the world might be saved through him" (John 3:16,17). The church as Christ's body, therefore, is God's partner in mission. There can be no denying it, no stepping aside from it. " 'Christ existing as community' (Bonhoeffer) is the church. It is the fellowship in which Christ lives, acts, and has acted in each moment of history since the Resurrection event."[4] In *Christ the Center*, Bonhoeffer presents the intriguing proposition that Christ is present as community and in the community, and further, that his only form between the Ascension and the Second Coming is the community.

The meaning of the church is debated by persons within and without. On the other hand, the church is seen and experienced as a very human instrument with numerous failings. On the other hand, as Baum observes, "The Church proclaims and embodies the Good News for all mankind. . . . The Church alone is conscious of the redemptive mystery that goes on everywhere."[5] The same writer quotes from an essay by Schillebeeckx:

> The Church reveals, proclaims, and celebrates in thankfulness the deepest dimensions of that which is being fulfilled in the world. . . . The Church is in fact the world where the world has come fully to itself, where the world confesses and acknowledges the deepest mystery of its own life, the mystery of salvation fulfilled through Christ.[6]

The nature of the church is set forth in the letter to the Ephesians when the writer says:

> ... we are to grow up in every way into him who is the head, in-
> to Christ, from whom the whole body, joined and knit together
> ..., when each part is working properly, makes bodily growth
> and upbuilds itself in love (Ephesians 4:15-16).

It is this interwoven community of faith which functions as
God's partner in mission. The Church is that fellowship of persons (*koinonia*) drawn together around Christ who seek to be
responsive to his spirit; the incarnation of Christ's continuing
witness in the world.

Mission is Given by God

The mission in which the church serves as God's partner is
given to it by God. It is bound up in the gospel and is articulated
in Jesus' statement to the disciples as recorded in Matthew
28:18-20:

> All authority in heaven and on earth has been given to me. Go
> therefore and make disciples of all nations, baptizing them in
> the name of the Father and of the Son and of the Holy Spirit,
> teaching them to observe all that I have commanded you.

The mission surely includes also the preaching of good news to
the poor, the proclaiming of release to the captives and recover-
ing of sight to the blind, and the setting at liberty of the op-
pressed, as identified by Jesus in the synagogue at Nazareth
(Luke 4:18-21).

The mission cannot be so narrowly drawn that it is reduced
to nothing but preaching and baptizing, though these are essential elements. Rather, it must be set within the context of the four
Gospels and the Book of Acts. Jesus' words in Acts 1:8 were
broadly based: " ... you shall be my witnesses in Jerusalem and
in all Judea and Samaria and to the end of the earth." The
church's role as God's partner in mission changes according to
the needs of those among whom it witnesses. This is to say that
mission must be done both according to the guidelines of scripture and in response to the current scene. The latter must not be
permitted to overshadow the former; neither should it be set
aside, for to do so would be to cancel out any possibility for rele-
vant witness.

The fact is, though, that some persons are quite satisfied to
carry on the mission much the same as they knew it in their
childhood. Whether that is in relation to congregational life at

home or to overseas involvements makes little difference. Such an attitude is equally deadly in both settings. By implication, it says that the mission for which the church exists is not sufficiently important to be done in ways that are in keeping with changing needs and circumstances.

Mission as Dialogue

Baum addresses this issue by calling the church to enter into dialogue with others, in light of the spiritual insights they have to share. If God is at work in the whole of humanity, " . . . the Church must listen to others before she may speak to them." Baum goes on:

> The Church must discern Christ's presence in the religions, the cultures, and the value systems that she encounters. Only after she has become aware of the wonderful things which, despite man's universal sinfulness, God has worked in other communities can the Church offer her own witness to Jesus Christ. Therefore, the Church's proper evangelical mission today is dialogue with other people, whether they be members of other religions or have no religion at all.[7]

Certainly there is precedent in Jesus himself for such a style of relating. When Nicodemus came to explore the idea of being born again, he found an open yet responsive listener:

> Rabbi, we know that you are a teacher come from God; . . . Jesus answered him, "Truly, truly, I say to you, unless one is born anew, he cannot see the kingdom of God." Nicodemus said to him, "How can a man be born when he is old?" (John 3:2-4a).

The reported conversation continues with considerable give and take. One thinks also of the rich young man who asked what he should do to inherit eternal life (Luke 18:18-25); or of Peter when Jesus asked three times if he loved him (John 21:15-19); or of the many encounters with the scribes and Pharisees.

The Gospels leave little doubt that teaching was a large part of Jesus' ministry. It was teaching, however, that included a great deal of listening, not just to words, but to the persons who spoke them. In that dialogue, God's mission was being accomplished. Baum, as we have seen, marks this as the key for mission today. Such dialogue, he insists,

> . . . is not a purely humanitarian endeavor leading to better public relations. . . . While God is redemptively present to

[persons] in every truly human conversation, we here consider a dialogue in which Christ is specifically mentioned. In the Church's dialogue with other religious traditions, the Gospel is openly sounded. Christian witness is present in dialogue![8]

Mission as Proclamation

It should be emphasized that the church is called not only to listen, but also to proclaim God's good news in Jesus Christ that gave it birth and provides its reason for being. "You shall be my witnesses . . . ," said Jesus (Acts 1:8b). Although spoken to the first disciples, it applies to all who would be his followers. Indeed, the nature of the gospel itself is proclamation. That is, it is the kind of happening that must be shared. The gospel is an invitation to mission even as it is a completion of mission to us. The gospel lays upon all who receive it the responsibility to bear witness to others. It is not a gift that can be selfishly hoarded, nor (as in Matthew 5:14-16) is it a light that can be covered. All of us are called to give witness to the faith that is in us, and we do that both through preaching and the verbal sharing of our faith, and through the acting out of that faith.

Having looked in some depth at both the church and its mission, we turn to the relationship by which God ties the two together. To be a partner with another derives from a series of Middle English, Anglo-French, Old French, and Medieval Latin words that are continued in the little used *parcener*, which refers to one of two or more persons who share an inheritance. It is not far, then, to *partner* which fits well the members of Christ's body. The word describes "A person who takes part or engages in some activity in common with another or others; sharer; associate. . . ."[9]

Partners and Stewardship

By creation, election, redemption, and self-giving, God has brought us into the church and, therefore, into a partnership in God's mission to the world. To put it in a single statement: *Our partnership is mandated by God* (whose mission is to all persons) *in Jesus Christ* (whose body is one and cannot be divided) *for the world* (that God created and loves). Partnership is both a matter of obedience and integrity: *Obedience*, in the sense that it is clearly the will of God who has called us to be partners in the process of creation and in the work of sharing the good news; *Integrity*, in the sense that it is the only way we can be true to the nature of Christ's body.

Partnership in God's mission, if it is to be effective, calls for partnership within the church. That is, if the church as Christ's body is one, so also is the church as institution. The whole mission of God cannot be done by any one expression of the church. The local fellowship must be strong and well-knit together, but not so fond of its own body that it becomes good for nothing but gazing into a mirror admiring its own build. Similarly, the regional and national units of the church need to recognize their own limitations and the special gifts and ministries of each other and of the individual congregations.

In a very real sense, Jesus' parable of the talents applies with special force to the church. It is the gospel which has been entrusted to the church. Without stretching the point beyond its limits, one could say that it is Christ himself for whom the church is responsible. It is this treasure which we have in earthen vessels (2 Corinthians 4:7). "For it is the God who said, 'Let light shine out of darkness,' who has shone in our hearts to give the light of the knowledge of the glory of God in the face of Christ" (2 Corinthians 4:6). As God's partner in mission, the church exercises stewardship over the most valuable gift of all.

If the church is to fulfill its responsibilities as partner in God's mission, individuals must take seriously their membership in the body. Within the total and all-inclusive task of stewardship, there comes for the Christian the practical necessity of sharing one's material possessions. According to one church's statement, "This will entail giving (1) for the support of the church; (2) for the furtherance of the gospel; (3) for a ministry of love in helping to supply the material needs of [others]. . . . "[10]

A group of stewardship leaders chose to put it this way:

> Responsible use of God's gifts includes the act of giving to his church for its ministry and mission a worthy portion of the time, money, and ability entrusted to us. We are moved to do this by gratitude to God and by the desire to answer his love, by loving our neighbors and serving their needs.
>
> In Jesus, we most clearly see God's love in action. We believe that through Jesus' life, teachings, and continuing presence, our lives are changed. One result of this change is our desire and ability to use our resources through the Church for enacting the gospel in word and deed.[11]

However one says it, the church will be rendered powerless and ineffective in its calling as God's partner in mission if it does not receive the strong support and participation of all to whom, as members of Christ's body, that mission is entrusted. The church extends far beyond our own congregations, but that is where it starts for all of us. Therefore, we will be involved as Christ's witnesses in our own Jerusalems where many of the needs are to be found. We will not stop there, however, but will find ways to reach out into the Judeas and Samarias and to the very ends of the earth; even, if need be in this age of space travel, to those yet unknown inhabited places beyond the earth.

Through other persons, through agencies of the church, through sister churches in other lands, through the generous giving of money, through our own direct involvements, we share in God's mission which is made known to us in the gospel and has come to life for us and for all persons in Jesus of Nazareth.

PART II

STEWARDSHIP: THE PASTOR'S ROLE

CHAPTER
6

MATCHING PERSONAL PRACTICE TO FAITH

In Part I of this study, we explored the stewardship idea from the perspective of faith. The purpose was to assist the reader in the process of thinking about, developing, and pursuing a theology of stewardship that is in keeping with the biblical witness. Since it is probable that seminary students, pastors, and congregational lay leaders alike have had limited opportunity to pursue the theology of stewardship, it seemed appropriate to devote five chapters to this side of the subject.

Part II of the study is offered as a guide for pastors and others who are prepared to accept responsibility as leaders in stewardship. It grows out of the recognition that stewardship is as practical and down to earth as life itself; further, that the leadership of the church must be able not only to think and articulate its theology of stewardship, but to embody it. A further role of the church's leaders, in this writer's view, is to see that stewardship, as set forth in Part I, is given its rightful place in the ministries of the church. It is the thesis of these chapters that while one person cannot do it all, the pastor has special responsibility to be a vigorous leader in stewardship. Leadership is a key function of leaders, though it is frequently avoided, as suggested by the subtitle of a book, *Why Leaders Can't Lead.*[1]

A Priority for Pastors

It is almost an axiom of local church stewardship that little of lasting significance will happen apart from pastoral support and involvement. The validity of this assertion can be tested against the reader's experience and against the experience of regional and national stewardship leaders. This is not to say that everything hangs on the pastor; we know it does not. It is to say, however, that stewardship cannot be chucked aside by the pastor to care for itself. By the nature of the case, stewardship rates a priority ranking in the pastor's list of things to do.

This applies both to the professional and personal lives of the pastor. For all Christians, and certainly for those who practice their calling in the set apart ministry, Christ is the center of life in very specific ways. If we accept the view which holds that the church today is Christ's living presence among us, then we who give our lives in service through the church will consider with great care what it means in our own lives to translate the centrality of Christ into everyday life.

Those for whom Christ is the focal point of life find perfect freedom in their service. For them, life style concerns are dealt with as a natural outgrowth of the faith relationship. Their approach is not one of modern asceticism in which they forego all that is enjoyable. Rather, it is one of ordering their lives in such a way that God's kingdom, as revealed in Christ, rules in them. This is not to say that food and drink and clothing (Matthew 6:25-33), or things in general, are inherently evil. Neither is it to say

> ... that our lives would be more Christian and our commitment to God truer if we would eliminate as many [things] as possible. Not at all; these things are to "come to you as well," and it is right and good that they do. The simple life is not to be equated with the least possible consumption of worldly goods and satisfactions. No, the point is that these things can be good—very good—if they are used to support man's relationship to God rather than compete with it.[2]

The issue comes down to human freedom and responsibility. How does one determine whether a particular item supports or competes with God in Christ, the center of the Christian's life? Surely, it is not done by having someone else decide, for that is to take the way of the puppet or the ventriloquist's dummy; it is irresponsible in that one avoids the necessity of wrestling through difficult questions. At the same time, the Christian can hardly make decisions in solitude, apart from the community. As Paul said to the Corinthians, "'All things are lawful for me,' but I will not be enslaved by anything" (1 Corinthians 6:12). A bit later in the same letter, he said: "Therefore, if food is a cause of my brother's falling, I will never eat meat, lest I cause my brother to fall" (1 Corinthians 8:13).

Putting Theory Into Practice

The easy-answer-to-hard-questions approach taken by some writers and pastors, and desired by some readers and parishioners, at best is a misreading of what is possible and at worst is plainly dishonest. Our purpose in this chapter is to raise some of the hard questions as these relate especially to persons called by the church to serve as pastors. The assumption is not that such persons are qualitatively different from others, but that their function places upon them special responsibility. Just as the flight crew of a jumbo jet cannot fly an airplane without keen awareness that their own safety and that of the passengers depends on their putting flight theory into practice at the controls, so must the pastor understand the necessity of matching personal practice to faith. The leadership function and integrity itself both require that belief be balanced with action.

One reason that theology is viewed with suspicion by some persons is that it is perceived as being irrelevant. It is seen not as a framework for understanding life or for living it, but as something quite apart from it. It is associated more with intellectual meanderings that have something to do with God—perhaps—than with life that has a lot to do with us. Preaching may arise from deep faith, but unless it stays close to where people are, it will have little effect and will be endured as a religious exercise which, for some reason, the pastor needs to perform.

The matching of personal practice to one's faith in matters of stewardship is the specific concern we are dealing with. All of our faith statements about stewardship in Chapters 1-5 will have a hollow sound unless they are allowed to live in what we do. We come, then, to an examination of ways in which faith and practice are put together in our own lives. The importance of relationship of God in Jesus Christ remains uppermost for the Christian and leads to obedience but, as one writer says,

> What obedience means in a given situation cannot always be determined ahead of time abstractly. Christian discipleship is a matter which needs to be hammered out on the anvil of life's ex-

periences. God treats us as maturing followers, not as slaves who have no choice but to carry out prescribed procedures.[3]

Principles for a Christian Life Style

Without going to the extreme of offering up ready-made answers, the same author identifies a number of principles for a Christian life style. "We are not called," he says, "to a life without guidance. Such a life would be a new bondage in disguise. We would then become slaves to our inner ambitions, to sensuality, to selfishness, . . . "[4] The guidance to which he refers comes to us directly from our faith. He has systematized it into a series of principles which one may use in working out answers to particular life style questions. Among the principles are the following:

> 1. We shall acknowledge that our supreme loyalty belongs to God. . . .
> 2. We shall regard all human beings as created by God and as loved by him. Consequently, we shall regard all human life as of supreme value.
> 3. We shall regard the earth as a God-given trust and shall strive to live in harmony not only with other human beings, but with our natural environment, the soil, the water, the air, the vegetation, animal life, and space. . . .
> . . . .
> 7. We shall maintain as much concern for practice as we do for doctrine. The ethical demands of the gospel shall be as much our concern as so-called "orthodoxy" of belief.
> 8. We shall not regard either sex as subordinate to the other, or as second class citizens in the kingdom of God.[5]

These principals do not lessen the hard work of deciding their implications for a life style appropriate to the Christian steward. They may, however, offer some clues or point to a process that could be useful. Guideline number three, for example, does not spell out the danger of polution or the wasteful use of water or the indiscriminate harvesting of timber. It does call all of these and more to our attention, however, by implication, and sets them within the context of the earth as a God-given trust for which we, and all its inhabitants, are responsible.

Other life style questions are addressed as persons arrange for housing and furnishings. There was a day when, because of low salaries paid to pastors and the nearly universal custom of providing a parsonage, little room was left for decisions about housing and furnishings. I can recall my childhood years in a parsonage. The house provided adequate shelter and was turned into a home by loving parents, but it had none of the extras we now take for granted. Salaries then were woefully inadequate, so that careful management was a requirement for survival. Although there are still some places where pastoral remuneration remains shockingly low, this no longer is the rule.

More and more pastors are receiving salaries that are in keeping with their needs and their training. No longer are pastors expected to subsidize the church budget by being paid at a cut rate. Consequently, as a group, pastors are experiencing at least some degree of financial security. This is becoming increasingly so for those who negotiate a living arrangement whereby they are able to build equity in their own home.

All of this, of course, means that instead of having a rather spartan life style imposed upon them as a result of poor employment practices, pastors and their spouses and families have the opportunity, within limits, to choose how they shall live. They may opt for simplicity in all areas, even to the point of eliminating some of the more common comforts and gadgets, or they may elect simplicity in certain areas so as to enjoy a degree of luxury in others. Whatever they do, it is fair to expect their actions to give evidence of their faith.

The question is not so much what is right as what is right for the persons involved? How does a given priority in terms of expenditure relate to the values that are held? Does the urge to have an item that can be purchased override both values and good judgment so that either money is not available for basic necessities or unwise indebtedness is incurred? "The starting place of stewardship [oikonomia] is in family economics. The two belong together."[6] Furthermore, whether as single persons, couples, or families, all of us are involved daily in the practice of both.

Jesus taught that "You cannot serve God and mammon" (Luke 16:13). In the Aramaic language of Jesus' day, mammon

> . . . meant wealth, property, money, and profit. Even though mammon was not to be served, yet Jesus never spoke disparagingly of it. He took it seriously. . . . Bread was important to Jesus. So were houses, boats, sandals, robes, and donkeys. He knew that possessions could be used for God's purposes.
>
> The danger comes when a person starts thinking that money and possessions have intrinsic or inherent value.[7]

Prudent management of financial resources calls for the making of a budget, but even the budget needs to be built on the basis of the values we hold as Christian stewards.

> Values are shown in what we freely choose from among real alternatives, in what we prize and cherish, and in our consistent actions. . . . They are mixed with feelings, beliefs, and one's worldview.[8]

Our use of money provides a reliable index of our values. A review of one's checkbook or other expenditure records will leave little doubt about one's operative values. Excellent resources are available for those who wish to pursue this topic.[9]

Christian stewardship, as we have seen, includes all of life. In our money economy, however, the stewardship of financial resources looms large in the overall task of managing God's good gifts. Research conducted in the early 1970s showed that clergy,

> . . . who on the average are paid less than lay people, contributed nearly three times more than they do. A clergyman in the United States earns a median salary of $10,111 annually compared to the $11,075 earned by an average lay person, but the minister donated a median $14.65 a week, compared to the $5.52 given by the lay member. . . .
> . . . The more theologically versed clergy see the immediate tie between espousing faith in principle and backing it through receipts of their labor, a connection that lay people don't seem to grasp so fully.[10]

This is not cited as justification for the smugness some clergy may feel, but only as an illustration of the need for bringing faith and practice together. Informed estimates in one denomination indicate that on the average, members are giving only 2.6 percent of their income to the church in its several manifestations. There are many other national church bodies for which this would also be true. What does this say about the persons who promised to support the church with their prayers, presence, substance, and service? An average of two and one half percent does not seem very substantial!

Stewardship of Financial Resources

"Money giving," says the well-known psychiatrist Menninger, "is a good criterion of a person's mental health. Generous people are rarely mentally ill people."[11] The image that comes to mind is the transformation that takes place in Scrooge when he catches the spirit of Christmas and begins to discover the joys of sharing. The old penny-pinching miser allows his hardened crust to be punctured so that his own humanity is able, at last, to get out and the warmth of human friendship to get in.

The reader is encouraged to take a sharp look at current personal stewardship practice. If the percentage level of giving to the church is not known, it should be determined. One needs also to decide whether the percentage is figured in relation to gross income or after-taxes income. Whatever the percentage, the question that needs to be addressed squarely can be put simply: Does this level of giving represent a generous response to God, or is it calculating and tight-fisted? Is it in keeping with the values one holds and the faith one proclaims, or is it in conflict with one or the other?

Giving to the church stands as only one part of stewardship, which must be seen in relation to the whole of life and to other money-related concerns. One needs to guard carefully against the rich young man syndrome to which we all are subject.

> Faithful Christian stewardship is not easy to practice. We are constantly in danger of being seduced by covetousness, which is the idolatrous worship of money and material possessions.... Our world insists that a person's life does, in fact, consist in the abundance of possessions.[12]

The issue of stewardship in life is one major element in getting faith and practice together. Another that is overlooked or sidestepped by many persons is the question of stewardship in death. If we take seriously our responsibility in life to be careful managers of the blessings we receive, it seems strange indeed that we would consider ourselves free of such responsibility as life comes to an end. Those who work closely with the survivors of persons who practiced good stewardship faithfully in life do not grow accustomed to the knowledge that those same persons proved quite irresponsible in death. The importance of a properly executed will, one that reflects the values and faith of the deceased, can hardly be overemphasized, especially when a spouse or children are involved.

No one is in the position of being able to tell another what kind of clothes to wear, which car to buy, how expensive a house to live in, where the thermostat should be set, how much to spend for groceries or entertainment, or how much to give to the church.

Least of all should pastors make the mistake of handing out advice to others on the pretext of superior knowledge, since we know better and so do they. The *raising* of such questions with others is very much in order, however, and the answering of them for ourselves is required as we match personal practice to our faith.

CHAPTER
7

A CONTINUING PRIORITY
IN THE CONGREGATION

The focus in this chapter shifts from the individual to the congregation. This is not to imply that the two are unrelated or that there can be a neat separation between them. The distinction is made only for purposes of discussion and emphasis but should not be taken lightly. There is a blending of one into the other, however, as can be seen in the pastor as individual who is called to match personal practice to faith and the pastor as congregational leader/enabler who is responsible for assisting the congregation in developing an adequate stewardship program.

Pastoral Leadership is the Key

There are those pastors who pride themselves on not getting involved in stewardship. Some choose such a course, perhaps, because it is the way of least resistance; to say that they choose it may be less accurate than to say that they drift into it. Others may avoid stewardship because they have what they judge to be more important calls upon their energy and really do not want to be bothered. Still others may feel inadequate and ill-prepared to offer leadership in this area, therefore deferring to others.

It is the hope that readers of these pages, if they have been uncertain about the pastoral role in stewardship or have been hesitant to exercise it, will come to a vision of themselves and the pastoral office that will bring both clarity and courage. Part I of this study is aimed at engaging the reader in thoughtful theologizing about stewardship and is seen as a kind of foundation on which a program for the local church can be built. It is intended to make the case for a pastor's deep and continuing participation in stewardship concerns on the basis that stewardship is bound up inextricably with faith and life.

If stewardship is not seen by the pastor as a priority, it will have a difficult time and likely will not be given priority status by the congregation. Whether this is as it should be may be questioned, but the accuracy of the observations has been confirmed by stewardship colleagues in many communions. This is *not* to say that a congregation will be unable to generate enough money to keep itself going if the pastor is not in there pitching. It is to say, rather, that if biblical stewardship is to be understood and practiced in the church, the pastor's leadership will be a key to its happening.

The point of view being advanced here is that, by the very nature of the pastoral calling, we cannot evade the task of building up the *oikos*, God's household. The "living stones" of 1 Peter are the persons among whom a pastor ministers in response to the call of God and for the purpose of contributing to their growth and development. As they are built up and strengthened individually, they take their place as solid members in the wall of God's house. Their stewardship has both individual and corporate dimensions. According to one writer,

> ... corporate stewardship implies a certain view of the Church, an ecclesiology. It assumes that the congregation possesses unity which derives not only from the common interests and commitments of its members, but also from the peculiar relationship of this group to its Head. ... So the unifying power at work in the Church constitutes the congregation, a group which by definition must function as a corporate entity or else it is not true to its nature and calling.[1]

The pastor, therefore, must function within the community of faith; and the church must be prepared to receive the ministry of one who has invested years of training in order to be equipped for that ministry. The pastor brings certain skills in relation to the Bible, congregational life, the care of persons, and making the connections between faith and the experiences of everyday living. These skills should be in a process of continuous development. They should also be recognized by the congregation so that they can be employed to the fullest. This is to suggest that mutual trust between pastor and congregation is essential to a relationship which fosters growth.

If stewardship as interpreted in the foregoing chapters is to be a continuing priority in the congregation, it will be the result of strong pastoral leadership combined with the congregation's clear understanding of its own identity. "Stewardship is no optional alternative for the congregation; it is the very stuff of its life together."[2] No congregation, if this is true, may keep stewardship locked up in some basement room, separated from its ongoing life. Yet the fact is that a large number of congregations do exactly that, some even to the point of sending unmistakable signals to the pastor that stewardship is posted territory that should not be invaded.

More often, however, it seems that stewardship is a victim of neglect rather than of outright mistreatment. It tends to get lost among many other concerns and may as well reflect the pastor's reluctance as the congregation's opposition. Where this is the case, one might suppose that it is indicative of a too narrow view that sees only money, not life, as the context for stewardship. Wallace Fisher puts the issue sharply when he says:

> The church's effective witness during the remainder of this volcanic century will depend substantially on its rediscovering and shaping its life to the biblical concept of stewardship.... If lay and ordained church people in the Protestant and Catholic churches continue to rely on budgets, promotional literature, manipulative techniques, shallow homilies, and, in some quarters, thinly veiled coercive measures for "doing stewardship," God, weary of a church that ignores *his* stewardship, may employ other means and other people to accomplish his liberating purpose.[3]

The Importance of Biblical Study

The same author takes a more positive stance in a later paragraph in which he develops the implications of biblical stewardship:

> It is Christ who persuades some church members to be servants of the Word rather than servants of self or class or institution.... Biblical stewardship is a life-style with the Cross as its center. The church must challenge, inform, and persuade its community to embody God's Word in the world if it expects to be a force in society rather than a fungus on it.[4]

Here, then, is an exciting task for the church, and one that should call forth every pastor's best efforts. If biblical stewardship is to be a priority in the congregation, the pastor will help to make it so.

Apart from serious study of the scriptures, stewardship will not be seen in its fullest dimensions. Brattgard underlines this when he says: "Our investigation [of the scriptures] has often given occasion for the statement that the Christian concept of stewardship has a *total* dimension."[5] It is imperative, therefore, that the pastor engage in careful study of the Bible, drawing upon skills of language, method, and interpretation, utilizing the best available commentaries and other writings, and being open to the moving of God's Spirit within oneself and through other persons. If stewardship is to be a priority in the congregation, then careful encounter with the biblical witness must be a substantial priority for the pastor. Biblical stewardship is an emphasis, but more than that, it is a *perspective*, a way of understanding and relating to life, so that the pastor's study of virtually any biblical passage will have stewardship overtones.

Biblical study is a first step in making stewardship a continuing priority in the congregation. It does not automatically follow, however, that study will lead to action. In many communions the pastor is identified both as the spiritual and executive leader of the congregation. This dual role may well be a mandate for the pastor to take initiative in bringing stewardship to priority status. Some pastors are much more effective as spiritual leaders than as executive leaders. This may reveal a certain discomfort with the image and reality of power which accompanies anything executive. It tends, however, to overlook the importance of *executing*, carrying out, or doing.

There is nothing inherently bad or manipulative about executive leadership. Indeed, it may be very good and surely is necessary. If it is lacking in a congregation, one would almost be forced to the conclusion that the pastor's spiritual leadership is much less effective than it might otherwise be. That is, inspiration and good ideas cannot accomplish much unless they are implemented. Executive leadership and sensitivity to persons are not mutually exclusive in theory and need not be so in practice.

The congregation's organization is another factor in making stewardship a priority. If there is no group that is assigned and takes seriously the task of stewardship development, it will be difficult for the pastor alone to make any major stewardship impact on the congregation. Therefore, one of the early steps in making stewardship a priority would have to be the finding or creating of such a group if none exists. Whether a new group or not, the pastor will need to relate to it so that persons might be helped to see stewardship as a broader concern than giving money to the church or counting the offering, as important as these are. According to Fisher,

> The church is true to its stewardship of the mysteries of God when, at its grass roots, it proclaims and teaches that Word and from its resources motivates its constituency to let Christ inhabit their persons and through them serve others in the world.[6]

This is to emphasize once more stewardship as a Christian way of life. The pastor and all other committed adults will recognize that the first task is to understand and practice Christian stewardship in their own lives. Secondarily, they will serve as examples or models for others. Specifically, persons who relate to the church's nurture program will need to be deeply committed to stewardship education. They will need to be aware of stewardship resources that can be used helpfully with curriculum materials. There will need to be careful planning so that all persons in the church face up to the claims of Christian stewardship in every area of life.

A Plan for Action

Assuming that the congregation does have adequate organization and that the pastor is prepared to function as spiritual and executive leader, what are some of the plans and actions that will help to make stewardship a continuing priority?

The task of training persons who are elected or appointed to the stewardship group in many congregations will belong to the pastor. Even though job descriptions may spell out the functions of a stewardship committee, it is all too customary for some of those functions to be left undone. Persons who have a knack for dealing with building maintenance problems or supervising financial administration sometimes are unable to appreciate the importance of ongoing stewardship education. This need not be the result of obstructionism but instead may only reflect the simple lack of training. With such a group the pastor might well negotiate an opportunity for some intensive work on the relationship between Christian stewardship and assigned responsibilities.

The pastor's role as teacher may find expression in other ways: in a church school study of stewardship, as the teacher of an evening course on some aspect of stewardship, as a resource person who brings biblical expertise to groups being led by another, and certainly in church membership classes which offer an excellent opportunity for dealing with stewardship, as reported by one pastor:

> Laying it on the line about what it means to be a committed Christian is part of the curriculum for our new member classes. . . . The people who come through the classes give, on the average, three times as much as the people who have not gone through the classes. Not because they are richer, but because they know what giving is all about.[7]

The fact that persons who have been in the church all their lives do not understand what it means to be God's stewards is strong enough evidence that careful training and long-term education are needed.

For the pastor who wants to make stewardship a priority, preaching will be a natural and useful tool in the process. While there are some pastors who say they have never preached about money and do not intend to, most pastors and seminary students who understand *biblical stewardship* see it as a subject that cannot be excluded from the ministry of the Word. While one can be critical of the annual stewardship sermon or series of sermons related to the enlistment of financial commitments, one can also be grateful that stewardship and preaching are at least put together then.

There is good reason to schedule sermons that deal directly with stewardship at other times in the year, perhaps at least quarterly. If one were to build a preaching schedule on the basis of the frequency with which Jesus spoke about money, four sermons a year would hardly suffice. It should also be noted that while it is quite true that stewardship involves much more than money, it *does* involve it. It is especially urgent in our money-oriented economy for pastors to preach about the stewardship of money. For too long the subject has gotten the once-over-lightly treatment; it deserves far more.

Money itself is perfectly neutral. It is neither good nor bad, yet it is very much with us. How we get it; what we do with it; why we want it: these are issues that we must deal with as Christians, and thus they are issues that pastors must address in their preaching. They are not the extent of what stewardship preaching should speak to, however. There is also the very large concern about the stewardship of creation, the earth, the air, the water, space. There is the issue of the millions who do not enjoy life's basic necessities, much less share in the wealth to which most Americans have grown so accustomed.

Another way in which stewardship may become a priority in the congregation is through the pastor's counseling ministry, particularly in premarital and marital counseling. Marriage has many stewardship implications that should be explored fully by both parties. The whole question of values is really a stewardship concern. Also very much a part of marriage is the care of persons—spouses, children, and others—an aspect of stewardship that has special meaning to all who choose to live in the household of faith.

Stewardship teaching in the church ought also to encompass a reality many persons would prefer to avoid, namely, death and dying. There are questions related to this part of the life cycle that need to be considered within the context of biblical stewardship. For example, "What disposition shall be made of my body? Do I want to express my concern for an unsighted person by donating the corneas of my eyes? Shall I make my silent contribution to persons in need and to medical science by donating all usable organs or by offering my body for research? What about my estate? How shall I continue even in death to provide for family members and support the mission of the church?" These are questions the pastor together with the congregation's stewardship group might raise in various ways. While individuals must come to their own answers, the process of seeking those answers is one in which we can share constructively together in the church.

The purpose of this chapter is not to set forth a prepackaged stewardship program, since careful attention must be given to the needs of a particular congregation. The purpose, rather, is twofold: first, to suggest that biblical stewardship should become a continuing priority in the congregation—not the only priority, but a continuing one; and, second, to identify and describe some specific ways by which the pastor, working with a stewardship group, can make that happen.

CHAPTER
8

THE ENLISTMENT PROCESS

One tendency of church leaders today may be to write off as the product of modern gimmickry the process by which financial support for the church's ministries is secured. By whatever name the process is known—Commitment Plan (CP), Every Member Enlistment (EME), Commitment Enlistment (CE), Every Member Canvass (EMC), Every Member Visitation (EMV)—there is evidence that its use in North American churches remains rather spotty. "Denominational program developers," according to one study, "doubt that it is properly carried out in any given year by more than ten percent of the local churches."[1] In one denomination, twenty-five percent of the congregations reported having some form of enlistment in 1977. Generous estimates in other denominations might go as high as forty or fifty percent. Even if these latter are accurate, however, what about the fifty or sixty percent that leave this tool of Christian stewardship untouched?

Is one to suppose that congregations without an enlistment effort have already arrived at an ideal level of stewardship in which a majority of members give at least ten percent of their income through the church? Might it be, on the other hand, that persons in many of those congregations prefer to wait for occasional special appeals in place of expressing their support of the church through a weekly or monthly commitment? There is reason to believe that some congregations avoid an enlistment program because it involves hard work. For others, there may be a certain amount of self-protection involved. Whatever the reasons, it is clear that a minority of congregations in many communions participate in an annual stewardship enlistment.

More than a few congregations have had their initial experience with an enlistment effort as part of a building program. There need be no negative judgment in the observation that the possibility of providing a much improved or totally new facility has been the occasion in many churches for a bold new step in financial stewardship. A large number of those same congregations, it should be noted, have turned those facilities into effective instruments of ministry. As building debts are paid off, enlistment programs continue and funds are channeled into increased allocations for outreach and witness. Individual members have been challenged in the process and have grown in life-changing ways.

Ideally, perhaps, it would not be necessary for persons in the church to confront one another about the need for giving financial and other kinds of support to the body of which each one is a part. To put this forth as a reason for not doing what needs to be done, both for the church and for the individual member, however, is to default on the rational powers God has given us. The truth is that as concerned Christians share with one another about that which is close to them, including their money, good things happen and the gospel comes to life. Surely this is not far from the meaning of the New Testament writer's admonition to " . . . stir up one another to love and good works . . . " (Hebrews 10:24).

The Corinthian Enlistment

One major portion of the biblical foundation for financial enlistment among Christian persons appears in 2 Corinthians 8 and 9. There Paul makes his case to the church at Corinth for their support of sisters and brothers who were victims of the famine in Judea. Rolston says that " . . . the way in which Paul relates his appeal to the meaning of Christianity is for us a superb example of the way in which other appeals can be related to the great heritage which all Christians have in Christ."[2]

Rolston's exegetical study of these two chapters from 2 Corinthians, though brief, is helpful in that it lifts out in summary fashion the key points made by Paul, as follows:

> 1. Proving the genuineness of your love (" . . . but to prove by the earnestness of others that your love also is genuine."

8:8)

2. The grace of giving ("We want you to know, brethren, about the grace of God which has been shown in the churches of Macedonia, . . . " 8:1)

3. A fruit of the spirit ("Now as you excel in everything . . . see that you excel in this gracious work also." 8:7)

4. Giving out of their poverty (" . . . their abundance of joy and their extreme poverty have overflowed in a wealth of liberality. . . . " 8:2)

5. Fellowship in ministering to the saints (" . . . begging us earnestly for the favor of taking part in the relief of the saints. . . . " 8:4)

6. The gift of themselves (" . . . but first they gave themselves. . . . " 8:5)

7. The example of Christ (" . . . though he was rich, yet for your sake he became poor, so that by his poverty you might become rich." 8:9)

8. Equality based on love (" . . . but that as a matter of equality your abundance at the present time should supply their want, . . . " 8:14)

9. Spiritual compensations (" . . . he who sows bountifully will also reap bountifully. . . . And God is able to provide you with every blessing in abundance, . . . " 9:6,8)[3]

Referring to this summary in an essay on "Biblical Sources of Stewardship," Willard M. Swartley has this instructive and thought-provoking observation:

> While these Pauline teachings are commonly appealed to as instruction in Christian stewardship, Paul's willingness to risk death in order to share the relief gift with the needy in Jerusalem is more rarely noted. By comparing Romans 15 and Acts 20-21, it is clear that Paul's determination to go to Jerusalem at the end of his third missionary campaign, even despite Agabus' prophecy that he would be bound hand and foot (Acts 21:7-14), was motivated by his all consuming desire to present the relief gift to the saints in Jerusalem (Rom. 15:31).[4]

Without pressing the analogy unduly, one might at least raise the question as to whether the enlistment of support for Christ's continuing ministry through the church today calls for any less dedication.

A Shared Responsibility

In light of the relatively few congregations that engage in serious programs of stewardship education which lead naturally to the making of commitments and the sharing of gifts, and in light of the low percentage of income given through the church for all purposes, those who serve as leaders in the church have responsibility to work at bringing about change. Assuming what has come before in this study—that Christ is the center of life; life is the context for stewardship; stewardship is the practice of faith; faith is God's gift to the church; the church is God's partner in mission; there must be a matching of personal practice to faith; and stewardship should be a continuing priority in the congregation—one can hardly escape the enlistment process as a logical and necessary next step. It is there, waiting to be done.

To ignore the enlistment is to pass by an oppportunity for significant pastoral care. Far too many persons in our churches tend to spiritualize their faith right out of life. There are those who somehow have failed to deal with faith as it is expressed in financial support for the church and its ministries. The every member enlistment provides the occasion which prevents such failures from becoming the rule. If we are members of the body of Christ and if the church is that body which continues the work of him who is its head, one can hardly imagine why any pastor should be hesitant about inviting persons to do what every church member has already promised to do.

If some pastors are hesitant to call for a process by which persons are confronted with the need to declare themselves, they are encouraged greatly in that hesitation by some lay leaders. The purpose here is not to assess blame but to consider ways by which growth and change may be brought about. Even in the absence of strong support from others, and especially under those conditions, the pastor's leadership is crucial. It can help to make the difference between a congregation that faces up to its opportunities and one that becomes fixated on its own survival. There are too many congregations that bemoan their financial difficulties but do nothing at all to deal creatively with them. A pastor who is sensitive to the potential and does not give in to pessimism can be a true prophet of the Lord.

In terms of potential, for example, it is helpful to secure from the public library the per capita and household income figures for a particular area. These can be used to determine the total income of a congregation and, when compared with the congregation's giving, the percentage of income given through the church. While this relies on averages, it is hardly based on guesswork. A much more reliable method is to ask persons to record anonymously their actual household incomes and their giving to the church. Most groups in which this method is used are surprised by the size of the income figure. The percentage given to the church speaks for itself. Frequently the potential for growth is immediately apparent and becomes the motivation for action.

Suggestions for Pastors

It was noted earlier that many congregations had their introduction to an enlistment program when they were considering a building program. Since church building campaigns are not generally repeated for a generation or two, something else must be utilized to facilitate the interest and support of members. Many congregations—though not nearly enough—have adopted some form of annual enlistment. Suppose you are pastor of a congregation that has neither a new building program nor an annual enlistment, What can you do?

First, you might want to make stewardship a shared concern on the basis of careful study of the scriptures. This can be done through preaching, teaching, and the established organizational structures, as described in chapter 7. *Second,* you can show the need for an enlistment as it relates both to the stewardship development of persons and to the ministries of the church. Special attention might well be given here to the ministries beyond the congregation and local community since these tend to be less visible, somewhat removed, and probably less well supported. *Third,* you can make a specific suggestion that, since good education leads to action, there be an enlistment. As in other situations, however, patience and cultivation are required. New ideas may not be received with as much enthusiasm as that with which they are offered. *Fourth,* learn with and from others as you provide training for enlistment leaders. Help them prepare for their work. *Fifth,* be sure to take full advantage of the experience and knowledge of others through personal consultation and utilization of available resources. Chapter 9 will deal more fully with this issue. *Sixth,* you can take the lead in making your own commitment. Whatever your response at this point, it will count for little unless it reflects the faith you profess from the pulpit and in conversation with others.

The introduction to the *Commitment Plan Handbook*, which was produced in 1973 by fourteen denominations, states the case well for an enlistment process in the local church:

> Money, today more then ever, represents each of us—our intellect, skill, and sweat all wrapped up in coin, paper, and plastic. Jesus said something about our being lights. He instructed each of us to take the wraps off our light and put it in a central place so that all can benefit from its illuminating rays. If our money is our life in coin, then it can become our light and can be used to move the darkness away from ourselves and others. Our money, given *through* the Church, used by its various agencies as they strive to provide light in a dark world, makes the giver the light and the message bearer.[5]

Perhaps it would be well to enter here the disclaimer that an enlistment program is not primarily a fund-raising technique but rather a ministry of the Christian community to one another for the purpose of edification [*oikodome* in the Greek New Testament], or building one another up in discipleship. Brattgard relates this idea to one which was explored in an earlier chapter:

> To be edified implies that one is being built up into the wall of God's "house," that spiritual building program which [God] himself is occupied with. It is in this connection that the expression "living stones" is used (1 Peter 2:5).[6]

God's "Building Program"

The thesis of this chapter is that the enlistment process is one means whereby God's "building program" is moved along. There is a great deal more at stake than the raising of a budget. Indeed, one might say that this is a by-product—and a very important one, but still a by-product—of something much more basic. In the Bible, Brattgard points out, " . . . the love which unites is the necessary prerequisite for edification. This implies that a living stone takes its place in the wall and takes on itself responsibility for the community."[7] It suggests, too, that the kind of caring for one another that leads persons in the church to participate in an enlistment effort is true to the biblical message. It is on this basis that the pastor is urged to take an active leadership role in the enlistment process.

The church is not engaged in fund raising but in "people raising," as some stewards like to say. They are right. People raising, however, is not an automatic process that just happens. The building of those living stones into the wall of God's house is God's work and it is done as we in the church receive and share the love of Christ. Some of that growth can come about as we engage in the process of deciding how we shall use the financial resources we have and, more to the point, to what extent we shall translate our faith and commitment into financial and other support for the church.

The enlistment is not an attempt to coerce persons into doing something they do not want to do. In the past and under the guidance of insensitive campaign directors, some congregations have had bad experiences in which persons were manipulated and pressured. That may be effective fund raising, though few defend it, but it is not acceptable as a method for doing Christian stewardship. Even the methods of good enlistment practices have been improved. For example, until the early 1970s the common expectation in virtually all church enlistment programs was that the commitment card would be filled out and signed in the presence of the visitors. The recommended procedure now is that, following the visit, the card is filled out and taken to church on dedication Sunday.

This is not to encourage a new kind of privatism but to assist persons in doing what they really want on the basis of some understanding of what it means to be a Christian steward. There are those congregations that are working at the enlistment process through groups who are encouraged to talk openly about the use of money both in relation to individual/family needs and the portion of income that is given through the church. Even in settings that include only the visitor and an individual or couple, there is opportunity for in-depth sharing about material resources. I can recall two occasions in recent years when I was a partner in such conversations. In both instances they were a source of lasting inspiration.

There is a debate among pastors and perhaps between pastors and lay persons regarding the role a pastor should play in the enlistment process. Should it be one of complete control? Should it be one of complete disengagement? Neither position, in the opinion of this writer, is desirable. There is no need for the pastor to take over the enlistment process; indeed, to do so would be to misuse the pastoral office which should be geared to the enabling of others. There are persons who can do the job well if they are enlisted. It may be at this latter point where the pastor can offer special help and encouragement. Enough has been written throughout these chapters concerning the importance of the pastor's support in the stewardship program that further comment on the posture of disengagement is unnecessary.

Enlistment Means Work

There is one fact about the enlistment process that bears underlining and it is that the enlistment means work. There is no way around it; the only way is through it. Shortcuts cannot be counted on and may lead to problems that could have been avoided. The existing guides for an enlistment do not offer an easy way out, nor can they, for there is none; all of them require significant time and effort. Such guides[8] do, however, provide excellent help. Stewardship education that culminates in a year by year enlistment is what is needed in the churches.

One pastor found the details of an enlistment program to be somewhat distasteful and tedious. But later, in an evaluation letter to a friend when the program was completed, he acknowledged that careful planning and attention to detail combined with a readiness for growth on the part of the congregation to produce a very significant increase in the number of persons who make commitments and a twenty percent increase in the amount pledged.

Fisher puts it well when he says:

> The general criticism of the every-member canvass is that it is casual rather than purposeful, formal rather than existential, cultural rather than biblical. The corrective is obvious: teach the visitors biblical stewardship and equip them to teach it in the parish. That is a never-ending task.[9]

It is, however, a task that in many congregations has not even been started. It is hoped that this will not be the case in your congregation.

The issue first of all is one of faithfulness. As good stewards of the gospel, pastors and congregational leaders will press boldly the claims of Christ, witness to his power in their own lives, and enlist others in a life of loyal service. In doing so, they will give of themselves and their resources as they have received, " . . . good measure, pressed down, shaken together, running over, . . ." (Luke 6:38).

CHAPTER
9

STEWARDSHIP RESOURCES
OF THE DENOMINATION

This chapter assumes the theological positions set forth in Part I of this study. It does not rehearse them in detail but builds upon them. The reader may want to review chapters 1-5 so that what is written here is seen within the context of faith, as was intended. In keeping with the oneness of Christ's body, it should be noted at the outset of this chapter that the topic takes into account the fact that a denomination's stewardship resources have an inherent ecumenical dimension. This will be explored more fully in the pages that follow.

A rationale for dealing with the subject as stated in the chapter heading above is provided by several authors, one of whom is Joseph C. McClelland:

> The denomination creates the program of stewardship for its congregations, providing instruction, encouragement, and direction. In this area it is the key, setting the tone for all its congregations and members. Here is where the same bureaucracy so criticized by us all may function as a good steward, pushing forward into new territory and bringing its denomination to greater service for the glory of God.[1]

Based on findings of the North American Interchurch Study, Johnson and Cornell offer this observation:

As the jointly spawned and nourished creature of the local churches, the denomination is their servant. It is shaped, supplied and directed by them in expectation of service in return. It is the instrument enabling them to act concertedly in many fields, both nationally and abroad, to carry on work cooperatively beyond their individual capability or reach.

In that role, the denomination also is expected to provide aid directly to the local churches, materials and resources that could not be adequately developed alone.[2]

I too, agree that regional and national expressions of the church need to respond to the needs of congregations, but they need also to respond to God's mission with program that local churches could never provide.

Having built a case for dealing with the subject of this chapter, the question might be raised as to why anyone in the church should be concerned about the help that is available from denominational offices. One writer's response is that:

The congregational *leitourgia* [worship] must combine with *diakonia* [service] if genuine stewardship is to be carried on. This is why stewardship cannot be adulterated into a mere challenging of members to support the local institution, to care for the plant as an end in itself. It is mission that provides the test: A group geared for mission to the community—local and larger—can justify spending money on itself insofar as this aids in preparation for mission.[3]

The material in Chapter 5 has special relevance here and may provide instructive commentary for this chapter, particularly at the point of the church's stewardship of the gospel.

A Case Study

Within one denomination there is a situation which might serve to illustrate and concretize what has been said thus far. Action was taken by the denomination's legislative body calling for a proposal on a per member giving goal to be brought to that body by the church's general board. Staff persons who picked up the assignment came quickly to the judgment that at least one far-reaching issue was involved, namely, the denomination's overall level of financial stewardship. It was clear to those staff persons that any proposal on per member giving for general church ministries which failed to take into account the current level of giving to the church—local, regional, national—and related institutions would be poorly founded and of little value.

Consequently, the initial assignment was set aside for the

moment in order to deal with the more basic problem of a denominational giving record that for many years had remained fairly static. It was determined that this would become the handle. With an average of only two and one half percent of income given through the church, it seemed unlikely that anything significant would be accomplished by a simple legislative action establishing a higher per member dollar goal for the general ministries of the denomination. Something radical was called for if real growth was to result. Therefore, the proposal that was developed started with the larger concern of the proportion of income given through the church and related institutions. It said that within a decade the denomination should double the percentage of member income given from two and one half to five percent. Only by doing so, or at least by increasing the percentage by some figure, could there be any reasonable hope for boosting the per member giving to the general fund beyond the most minimal increments.

The facts are that, when the pie is in a four-inch pan and there are six persons at the table, the only way to increase the size of the portions for all is to enlarge the pie to eight or nine inches. This is to take the holistic approach which is much more the biblical stewardship style than some other more institutionally self-serving models in which the primary concern is the funding of a single expression of the church, sometimes without regard to the others. Within such a framework, the setting of challenging per member goals for the general fund makes sense and may well contribute to the growth in financial stewardship on which it rests.

Whether the denomination involved in this example will accept the recommendation, to say nothing of whether it will achieve the ten-year turnaround, remains to be seen. For purposes of this chapter, the implications of the process just described are that while the denomination derives its existence from the congregations and depends heavily upon them, it also helps to share the life of congregations as they respond to actions and programs designed to move the church beyond the *status quo*. This is not to suggest that denominational staffs and organizations in and of themselves can accomplish the programs to which they give birth; only that they provide the overview and resources to the congregations as they go about tasks that are uniquely theirs.

The Pastor and the Denomination

There is something to be said about the role of a pastor in

relation to the denomination. By polity and by definition, pastors of congregations that belong to a denomination exercise their ministry within the disciplines of that denomination, however those disciplines may be administered. Persons who serve on regional and national staffs in many communions are keenly aware of the fact that some pastors not only are out of tune with the denomination but are playing in a totally different key and perhaps seeking to create their own independent orchestras. In more than a few instances this has resulted in painful congregational splits, costly litigation, and a loss of vision as to the church's reason for being.

The pastor sometimes is described as a gatekeeper, and there are legitimate reasons for such a description in congregations where the professional leader adopts a posture which is not supportive of the denomination. The pastor might just as well be seen, however, as the door opener, who works at the task of interpreting the denomination to the congregation and vice versa. If stewardship or any other resources of the denomination are to be utilized by a congregation, there must be awareness of their availability. In this, the pastor can be a great help by adopting and encouraging a stance which is both open and receptive to resourcing from the denominational office.

Many denominations prepare regular mailings to pastors for the purposes of keeping them informed in the various areas of congregational life—nurture, witness, celebration, stewardship—sharing ideas about ministry, and interpreting programs of the larger church. A problem uncovered in the North American Interchurch Study was that while pastors were seeing stewardship literature, a sizeable percentage of lay persons were not.

> Ninety-eight percent of the clergy had seen some, indicating an ample flow of material from denominations . . . to the pastors. However, only 61 percent of the laity reported ever seeing any such material. Somewhere between the national denominational offices and the local lay people, the information had been filtered out.[4]

On the basis of this finding, one denomination altered its approach to congregations so that both the pastor and the responsible lay leader in a given area now receive the mailings. The flood of mail across a pastor's desk is heavy and constant, so that one can readily understand how slippage was almost certain to occur under the old system.

Resources and Services

Against the background of pastoral ownership of denominational relationships and program, we turn now to a listing and description of stewardship resources and services available from the denomination:

1. *Annual stewardship packet.* Virtually every denomination provides pastors and stewardship chairpersons with a packet of materials geared specifically to the fall enlistment. These materials are developed around a theme which many denominations share in common. They include attractive posters; letterheads, mailing envelopes, self-mailers; presentation folders in which a congregation's program budget can be printed; leaflets, folders, and hangovers that interpret the theme and work at stewardship education; prayer/place cards that can be placed on the kitchen or dining room table; Sunday service folders, commitment cards, note cards. In addition, the packet offers a listing of study materials for various age groups, books that deal with many aspects of Christian stewardship, more specialized resources on Christians doing financial and estate planning, information of wills, life style, and basic enlistment resources. Such packets always come with suggestions as to how the various items may be used.

Many denominations are able to multiply the number of stewardship resources they provide by joining with one another through the Commission on Stewardship of the National Council of Churches. This group operates through a number of action teams composed largely of national stewardship staff persons. The teams deal with the practical need for materials and resources faced by the denominations and are responsive to that need. Without such cooperative efforts, all participating denominations would be somewhat deprived and many would find it impossible to provide their congregations with the necessary stewardship materials.

2. *Stewardship education resources.* Although mentioned above, it is important to note that stewardship belongs in a congregation's year-round educational plan. Denominational offices can suggest resources appropriate for children, youth, and adults. These range from full year curriculum materials to resources that are adaptable for a quarter or as few as four or six sessions.

3. *Stewardship training opportunities.* These may be in the format of national or area events. In one denomination, for example, both are offered, the former beamed toward the development

and assisting of regional leaders and the latter designed specifically for local church leaders. One retired couple experienced what could only be described as a stewardship conversion during one of the national seminars. They returned to their home area with the conviction that it was time for a major thrust in stewardship and with the commitment to help bring it about. As a direct outgrowth of their involvement, two regional seminars were held for churches in their area, with every participating congregation committing itself to at least two specific stewardship objectives to be undertaken in the two months that followed. These seminars were rooted in biblical and theological understandings of stewardship and were planned in close consultation with persons who identified pressing needs. One reason for the effectiveness of these regional events is the requirement that the pastor be present for the entire time, generally a weekend from Friday evening through Sunday noon, along with a minimum of four lay persons. Other training experiences may include such subjects as the making of a will, budget building and financial administration in the congregation, and workshops on congregational enlistment plans.

A growing concern among stewardship leaders, pastors, and lay persons in many denominations has to do with what is known variously as environmental stewardship, the stewardship of creation, and the care of the earth. Most denominational staffs have someone whose portfolio encompasses these concerns which are closely related to life style issues. As such concerns grow, they will likely be given more prominence among other denominational priorities.

4. *Denominational statements on stewardship.* These may be of limited value but they reflect the official position of the denomination and provide a framework for stewardship in the congregation. Pastors should be familiar with such statements which may be secured from the appropriate denominational office.

5. *Consultations and field assignments.* By means of correspondence and the telephone, every pastor has access to denominational stewardship staff in national or regional offices. Such persons are eager to assist pastors and local lay leaders. They give thoughtful attention to requests for help and are able to provide desired information. Frequently, requests for on-site consultations can also be met, though in the case of national staff time limitations may restrict participation to events which involve a number of congregations. This need not deter pastors from seeking assistance and, in fact, may become the occasion for

one congregation's sparking interest in others.

Some denominations have staff who are available to assist congregations in their enlistment efforts. Even denominations that do not have such staff arrangements often have helpful information about qualified persons who are prepared to render such service on a drive-in or other short-term basis.

6. *Clearinghouse on stewardship ideas and programs.* Denominational offices are eager to hear from pastors about fresh approaches that have been tried and new ideas still in the process of development. Most national stewardship officers have access to communications channels with pastors and local stewardship leaders and are regularly on the lookout for helpful stewardship suggestions that may be shared with others. To illustrate, one congregation studied the matter of bequests and adopted a policy as a guide for itself and for persons who may wish to include the church in their will. The paper was circulated by the national stewardship staff to pastors and local stewards chairpersons as an example of how one congregation chose to deal with what could be a difficult problem. It is reasonable to assume that, as a result of this sharing, a number of churches were motivated to establish their own bequest policy and that, in doing so, they made use of the model.

7. *Ecumenical linkages.* It is right, both from theological and practical perspectives, that those who minister on behalf of Christ's church on national stewardship staffs should work closely with one another. While this may occur spontaneously and informally, it is more likely to happen on a continuing basis through a regularized channel such as the Commission on Stewardship. In addition to the materials produced for the denominations, the Commission is a spawning ground for new ideas. It is also a transformer of dreams into realities. One example is the Ecumenical Stewardship Resource Center, a seminary based training and resource center in the process of being launched, whose purpose is to offer training in stewardship for laypersons, clergy, and those called to special stewardship ministries, and to encourage study and research in the field. Stewardship staff persons in the sponsoring denominations can provide detailed information.[5]

A former stewardship executive says:

> Denominational structures are Christ's instruments to the extent that they are responsive to the leading of his spirit and are responsible in their leadership. On the one hand they must

make way for the Holy Spirit to become real in their objectives and sense of direction and, on the other hand, under his guidance they must employ the most responsible methodology which human ingenuity can devise. This is stewardship at its best.[6]

Stewardship functions are incorporated into the structure of every denomination and nearly every one has professional staff who carry those responsibilities. Far from being enemies of the local church and the pastor, these persons are among their strongest supporters. They have a vision of the church which keeps the congregation in full view and sharp focus. They are committed to a theology with Christ at the center of life, all of which is a gift held in trust. They are among the resources a denomination makes available to the churches. Whether clergy or lay, they minister in God's household as stewards of the good news.

There is one additional consideration that must not be overlooked. It has to do with the pastor's role in helping to assure that the denomination will continue to have stewardship and other resources. To put it plainly, it has to do with the congregation's financial support of the denomination and its response to the call of Christ to go into all the world. Whether such support is by the congregation's self-allocation, as in some communions, or by assessment, as in others, the attitude of the pastor is crucial. If the denomination is viewed with suspicion and distrust rather than with appreciation and confidence, the financial support is likely to be minimal at best.

The person who is granted the privilege to function as a pastor has the responsibility on theological, ecclesiastical, and organizational grounds to be supportive of the denomination within which that ministry is exercised. This responsibility is not discharged by being neutral on the matter of denominational support, certainly not by urging the church to channel its support away from the denomination and into independent projects. It is carried out, rather, by seeing and presenting the ministries of the denomination as an extension and enlargement of the congregation's mission and by facilitating the solid financial support of those ministries.

NOTES

INTRODUCTION

1. "Data Report, Seminary Stewardship Education Survey" (New York: Commission on Stewardship, National Council of Churches, 1976, distributed with a letter from Nordan C. Murphy, 6 October 1976).

CHAPTER 1

1. Bonhoeffer, Dietrich, *Christ the Center* (New York: Harper and Row, 1966), p. 64.
2. Ibid., p. 62.
3. Ibid., pp.96-98.
4. Dietrich Bonhoeffer, *Ethics* (New York: Macmillan Co., 1970), p. 58.
5. Robert V. Moss, quoted in George S. Siudy, Jr., "What is Stewardship Today?", *A.D.,* October 1977, p. 45.
6. Ibid., p. 46.

CHAPTER 2

1. Siudy, "What is Stewardship Today?" p. 45.
2. "Hoeffer Seeks Relaxed Plastics Rules," *Elgin Daily Courier-News*, 14 July 1978, p. 13.
3. Produced by the Lutheran Brotherhood, Minneapolis; available from denominational or judicatory offices.
4. Brother Lawrence, *The Practice of the Presence of God* (New York: Fleming H. Revell, 1895), p. 13.
5. Ibid., p. 30.

6. *Church Financial Statistics and Related Data 1978* (New York: Commission on Stewardship, National Council of Churches of Christ, 1978), p. 13.

7. *World Peace Tax Fund Bill* (Washington: National Council for a World Peace Tax Fund, folder, n.d.), p. 5.

CHAPTER 3

1. Helge Brattgard, *God's Stewards*, trans. Gene J. Lund (Minneapolis: Augsburg Publishing House, 1963), pp. 22-24.

2. Ibid., p. 26.

3. John Reumann, "Stewards of God—Pre-Christian Religious Application of Oikonomos in Greek," *Journal of Biblical Literature*, Vol. 77, pt. 4 (1958).

4. Brattgard, p. 32.

5. Ibid., p. 37.

6. Ibid., p. 38.

7. Ibid., p. 44.

8. Ibid., p. 48.

9. Edwin A. Briggs, ed., *Theological Prespectives of Stewardship* (Evanston: General Board of the Laity, Division of Stewardship and Finance, 1969), p. 130.

10. Wallace E. Fisher, *A New Climate for Stewardship* (Nashville: Abingdon, 1976), p. 20.

CHAPTER 4

1. Briggs, p. 7.

2. Ibid.

3. Brattgard, p. 150.

4. Ibid., p. 151.

5. Alan Richardson, ed., *A Theological Word Book of the Bible* (New York: Macmillan, 1951), p. 75.

6. Gregory Baum, *Man Becoming* (New York: Herder & Herder, 1970), p. 41.

7. Warren F, Groff, "A Congregational Meditation" (Elgin: Church of the Brethren General Board, Peace Message #2, 1978), p. 2.

8. Fisher, p. 33.

CHAPTER 5

1. Emil Brunner, *I Believe in the Living God* (Philadelphia: Westminster, 1961), p. 127.

2. Richardson, p. 46.

3. Brunner, p. 135.

4. Fisher, p. 29.

5. Baum, pp. 63-64.

6. Baum, p. 63, quoting "Christian Faith and the Future of the World," *The Church Today*, p. 82.

7. Baum, p. 81.

8. Ibid., p. 83.

9. *Webster's New World Dictionary* (Cleveland and New York: World, 1968), p. 1067.

10. "Statement of the Church of the Brethren on Tithing and Christian Stewardship" (Elgin: Church of the Brethren General Board, 1963), p. 5.

11. "Stewardship for Our Time" (Philadelphia: United Church of Christ Stewardship Council, folder, 1974).

CHAPTER 6

1. Warren Bennis, *The Unconscious Conspiracy: Why Leaders Can't Lead* (New York: AMACOM, 1976).

2. Vernard Eller, *The Simple Life* (Grand Rapids: Eerdmans, 1973), pp. 28-29.

3. D. George Vanderlip, "Discovering a Christian Life Style," *Eastern Baptist Bulletin*, November 1977, p. 3.

4. Ibid.

5. Ibid., pp. 3-4.

6. Nordan C. Murphy, ed., *Christians Doing Financial Planning* (n.p.: Commission on Stewardship, NCCUSA [sic], 1976), p. 3.

7. Ibid., pp. 3-4.

8. Ibid., p. 5.

9. The reader is referred especially to *Christians Doing Financial Planning* which includes an Economic Value System exercise.

10. Douglas W. Johnson and George W. Cornell, *Punctured Preconceptions* (New York: Friendship Press for the Section on Stewardship and Benevolence, NCCCUSA, 1972), pp. 137, 139.

11. Quoted in Martin E. Marty's *Context* (1 July, 1977), pp. 5-6, from *The Lutheran*.

12. Murphy, p. 3.

CHAPTER 7

1. T.K. Thompson, ed., *Stewardship in Contemporary Life* (New York: Association, 1965), p. 93.
2. Ibid., p. 95.
3. Fisher, pp. 13-14.
4. Ibid., p. 15.
5. Brattgard, p. 193.
6. Fisher, p. 41.
7. Quoted by Robert J. Hempfling, "The Minister's Role in Stewardship Promotion," *Church Finance Council Minister's Bulletin*, August-September 1978, p. 2.

CHAPTER 8

1. Johnson and Cornell, p. 157.
2. Holmes Rolston, *Stewardship in the New Testament Church*, rev. ed. (Richmond: John Knox, 1963), pp. 83-84.
3. Ibid., pp. 84-87.
4. Willard M. Swartley in Mary Evelyn Jegen and Bruno Manno, eds., *The Earth Is the Lord's* (New York: Paulist, 1978; paperback), p. 36.
5. Nordan C. Murphy, *Commitment Plan Handbook* (n.p., 1973), p. 5.
6. Brattgard, p. 28.
7. Ibid.
8. See especially *Commitment Plan Handbook* and *Commitment Plan Guidelines for the Smaller Congregation*, both available from denominational stewardship offices. A new enlistment guide (working title: "Commitment Plan for Today") is currently being developed by the Commission on Stewardship of the National Council of Churches of Christ in the U.S.A. Additional information on this resource may be found in Appendix A, Stewardship Resources for the Pastor, no. 4 on p. 100.
9. Fisher, p. 117.

CHAPTER 9

1. Thompson, p. 123.

2. Johnson and Cornell, p. 100.

3. Thompson, pp. 101-2.

4. Johnson and Cornell, p. 100.

5. List of participating denominations is available from the Commission on Stewardship, National Council of the Churches of Christ in the U.S.A., 475 Riverside Drive, New York, N.Y. 10027.

6. Thompson, p. 188.

APPENDIXES

APPENDIX A

STEWARDSHIP RESOURCES
FOR THE PASTOR

1. *A Stewardship Bibliography*

This publication of the Commission on Stewardship of the National Council of Churches was brought out in 1976 for fifteen participating denominations. Updated annually in the Commission's *Journal of Stewardship*, the bibliography is carefully annotated. Entries appear under six headings (number of entries is shown in parentheses):

> General and Theoretical (23)
> Practical Stewardship (13)
> Ecology, Environment, and Eco-Justice Concerns (18)
> Financial Management: A. Personal and Family (10)
>   B. Corporate and Church(4)
> Wills and Special Gifts (24)
> Stewardship Books for Young Readers (8)

The bibliography is described as " . . . a working list, contributed by stewardship executives who work together in the Commission on Stewardship. They have found these books to be useful in their own work and in the stewardship life of the churches they serve." This is an excellent, well-rounded bibliography with annotations that will help pastors identify materials they want to utilize.

Persons in the following denominations who wish to secure

the bibliography should contact their national stewardship office:

American Baptist Churches, U. S. A.
The American Lutheran Church
Christian Church (Disciples of Christ)
Church of God (Anderson, Indiana)
Churches of God, General Conference
Church of the Brethren
Lutheran Church in America
The Lutheran Church - Missouri Synod
Moravian Church in America, Northern Province
Presbyterian Church in Canada
Presbyterian Church in the U. S.
Reorganized Church of Jesus Christ of Latter Day Saints
United Church of Canada
United Church of Christ
The United Methodist Church

Others should contact the Commission on Stewardship, 475 Riverside Drive, New York, New York 10027.

2. *Annual Stewardship Calendar*

A sample calendar prepared by one denomination will serve to highlight the scope of local church stewardship concerns and to indicate how they might fit into the calendar for a year. The sample follows:

1979 CALENDAR FOR STEWARDS

Early in the year, it is important to take an overview of what the Commission of Stewards need to do in the next 12 months. Besides reading this yourself, you may wish to make it an item for your commission agenda this month. Consider also the possibility of providing each commission member with a copy. Another idea: Look at this calendar at each monthly meeting and work ahead so as to have adequate time for implementing program.

January   Review the work of the commission. Make sure new members are given sufficient orientation—playing catch-up is no fun.

Stewardship Education
—Study units on stewardship
—Lifestyle/Christian values workshops
—Personal and family financial planning
—Commitment plan
—Will/estate planning

Church property
—Custodial care
—Maintenance (Don't overlook or procrastinate parsonage needs)
—Protection, insurance

Finance
—Annual budget building
—Handling the churches money; *special concern:* cash management
—Supervision of the treasurer and financial secretary
—Regular reporting of receipts and disbursements to the board and congregation

February 4   SHARE Interpretive/Offering Emphasis.

March 25   One Great Hour of Sharing Interpretive/Offering Emphasis.

Arrange with the pastor for a member of the Commission of Stewards to meet with the class for new members. Invite them to make a commitment of money and service when they are received into membership.

April   Encourage the church board to begin the goal setting process for 1980 program in order to facilitate budget planning in the fall. Resource: Congregational Goals Discovery Plan.

Beat the rush by naming the coordinator/chairperson for the fall enlistment by April 30. Be prepared to order necessary resource materials.

May   In preparation for the fall enlistment, initiate a study of giving patterns in your congregation.

Stewardship Packet will be mailed this month to pastors and stewards chairperson.

June 3   Annual Conference Interpretive/Offering Emphasis.

Become familiar with the contents of the annual Stewardship Packet.

July 3-8   Annual Conference, Seattle.

Order Commitment Plan resources, "Help Fulfill God's Purposes—Give" theme materials, offering envelopes.

August   Continue planning for fall enlistment. Complete the task of arranging for and securing leadership.

Begin the process of building a challenge budget in consultation with the board and based on program goals for next year.

September   Complete plans for the fall Commitment Plan for the enlistment of financial and human resources.

Look behind and ahead to make sure plans and follow-through are on schedule.

September and October — District Partners in Mission training events.

October 7   World Mission Interpretive/Offering Emphasis.

Plan for local Partners in Mission interpretation in cooperation with the board.

October and November — Engage in the Commitment Plan.

November   Complete the 1980 budget proposal for consideration by board and congregation.

Return 1980 Partners in Mission report.

Make plans for achieving the budget requirements for 1979.

November 18 — Bethany Theological Seminary offering.

Stewardship Dedication Sunday.

December 1   Be certain that Partners in Mission reports have been returned to district and Brotherhood offices.

23   Christmas/Achievement Interpretive Offering Emphasis.

24   See that all financial obligations of the congregation, including outreach, are cared for.

3. *Annual Stewardship Packet*

This item is provided by denominational offices to pastors and/or local stewardship leaders. Generally, it includes samples of materials available for fall enlistment programs. These are keyed to the annual theme which, along with the materials themselves, is developed cooperatively by national stewardship leaders representing many denominations. A listing of other stewardship resources (e.g., books, study guides, audio-visuals, wills and estate planning materials) is to be found in these packets. Suggested use: Pastors should become familiar with the contents of the packet, discuss them with stewardship leaders so that planning for the year can anticipate needed resources, and file.

4. *"Commitment Plan Handbook" and "Commitment Plan Guidelines for the Smaller Congregation"*

The first of these is the basic resource for congregations wanting to conduct an effective stewardship enlistment program. As the title of the second implies, it is based on the *Commitment Plan Handbook* but is modified according to the needs of smaller congregations. The *Handbook* is the most helpful resource currently available. It was published in 1973 and was the product of cooperative development through the National Council of Churches Commission on Stewardship. Fourteen denominations in the U. S. and Canada participated. The *Handbook* provides detailed guidelines for all aspects of local church enlistment. Many congregations have found this resource to be helpful and effective. Although the home visit is presented as the norm, an accompanying booklet (*Commitment Plan Handbook Modules,* sold with the

Handbook itself) offers a number of other methods that have been tried and tested. Order from denominational offices.

As of this writing, a replacement for the *Handbook* is in the early stages of development under the tentative title, "Commitment Plan for Today." This is to be focused on congregations of 200 members or less, with necessary instructions and resources for adaptation to larger congregations. The format is to be loose-leaf cards. This resource should be available for use by local churches during the fall of 1980. Information will be forthcoming from denominational stewardship offices.

5. *"Church Financial Statistics and Related Data"*

This is an annual publication of the National Council of Churches Commission on Stewardship and distributed to pastors and others by many denominational stewardship offices. The booklet includes:

> Information that provides for comparison of local church giving in the several denominations
>
> Analyses of giving
>
> Information on individual, family, and household income that can be used in the development of financial resources potential
>
> A breakdown of average family expenditures and overall consumer spending
>
> Articles dealing with very practical concerns such as how inflation affects per capita giving (this resource is usually available in the fall from denominational stewardship offices)

6. *Ecumenical Stewardship Resource Center*

This cooperative venture is under the sponsorship of the Commission on Stewardship of the National Council of Churches and involves denominational stewardship offices and theological seminaries. The purpose of the Center as set forth in the proposal " . . . is to provide a locus where appropriate research, planning, resourcing and implementing designs can be developed that will: (1) Interface the various disciplines that relate to the issue . . . ; (2) Provide a central base for research and resource development . . . ; (3) Provide an international network of teaching/learning locations . . . ; (4) Equip persons in ministry, both academically and programmatically, to function competently as stewards and teachers of stewardship within their assigned fields; (5) Facilitate an analysis of historic and cross-cultural patterns of financial support of the church . . . ; (6) Study and provide resources which delineate the relationship of the Christian faith to capitalism, socialism, and welfare state policies . . . ; (7) Intensify effort to relate theoretical studies to the concrete needs of the church." It is hoped that the Center will become operational in 1980. Information may be secured from denominational stewardship offices.

7.   *"Handbook for: Christians Doing Financial Planning"*

This paperback publication of the Commission on Stewardship of the National Council of Churches is a do-it-yourself guide for individuals and families. It provides guidelines on values clarification, goal setting, and budgeting. In addition, helpful information is presented on insurance, credit, wills, and record keeping. The *Handbook* also lends itself to use in group workshops on financial planning. It is available from denominational stewardship offices. A fun exercise which the writer has done: Spouses fill out the values clarification forms independently and then use the results as a basis for discussion of their own relationship.

8.   *"Journal of Stewardship"*

This sixty-four page booklet is produced annually by the Commission on Stewardship of the National Council of Churches. It is prepared especially for local church pastors and other church leaders concerned with stewardship in all its aspects. The *Journal* is both provocative and practical. It is one of the musts for the pastor's shelf. It is provided free to pastors by some denominations. For those who must pay, the cost is minimal. Available from denominational stewardship offices. Note that the *Journal* for 1978 includes on pages 57-64 an updating of *A Stewardship Bibliography* (number one on page 95). Entries are categorized and annotated.

9. *Stewardship Study Materials*

Denominational stewardship offices can recommend materials for use in church school classes, study and discussion groups. Some cover as few as four sessions to as many as thirteen or more. Order forms in annual stewardship packets include listings of such resources.

APPENDIX B

"A FAITH VIEW OF STEWARDSHIP"

A Seven Session Study Course

Overall Purpose:

To provide an outline for a seven-session course on stewardship designed to look at the biblical and theological bases of stewardship. This will involve persons in Bible study, sharing, discussion, and thought which will contribute to the participants' being able to articulate their own theology of stewardship. Each of the sessions is planned for a two-hour time block. One of the most helpful resources for this study is the book, God's Stewards, *by Helge Brattgard (available from denominational stewardship offices and/or bookstores).*

SESSION 1 — "Christ Is the Center of Life"

A. *Purpose:* To set Christian stewardship in the broad context which starts with commitment to Christ as the center of life.

B. *Objectives for the Session:*

1. Facilitate the developing of the group with a life expectancy of seven weekly sessions.

2. Secure a brief written statement from each participant regarding his/her understanding of stewardship.

3. Provide an overview of the course outline and move into the first topic.

C. *Teaching Plan:*

1. Introductory comments and opening sharing. Ask each person to share one significant experience or happening from the last seven days.

   Text: "In an adult class the student's experience counts for as much as the teacher's knowledge." (Quoted in Knowles, *The Adult Learner*, page 84.)

2. An overview of the course.

   a. Leader identify the issues to be considered.

   b. Opportunity for group reactions, input, expectations.

3. Have each participant prepare a brief written statement on "My Understanding of Stewardship."

   Purpose: To help teacher and participants know where persons are in their understandings so as to have guidance for discussion and a base for comparing at the end of the course.

4. Introduction of topic for Session 1.

   a. Suggested reading: *Christ the Center* by Dietrich Bonhoeffer; Chapter 1 of this book, "Christ Is the Center of Life."

   b. Consideration of what it means to have Christ as center.

5. Bible Study.

    a. Working in small groups, explore for stewardship ideas some of the best-known stories of the Old Testament, with sharing later in the total group. List stewardship discoveries on chalk board.

Eliezer and Abraham	Genesis 24:1-27
Joseph and Pharaoh	Genesis 39-41
Moses and God	Exodus 3-4

    b. Consider New Testament accounts in light of Christ as center.

Ephesians 1:3-14; 3:4-6	Colossians 1:15-20
Philippians 2:1-11	

6. Sharing of insights, inspirations, questions.

7. A look at the topic for Session 2.

Suggested readings: The Creation stories; Gospel accounts of Jesus' stories, encounters with others concerning money, property, talents; Acts 5:1-11.

SESSION 2 — "Life Is the Stuff of Stewardship"

A. *Purpose:* Building on the study of Christ as Center, focus on life in all its aspects as the way we do our stewardship.

B. Objectives for the session:

1. Recap the study of Session 1, drawing on the group in the process; review Chapter 1 of this book.

2. Sharpen the focus of the session so that persons will be stimulated to think of crossing points with their ex-

perience; provide opportunity for sharing.

3. Introduce the holistic approach to stewardship as set forth in the Creation stories, the parables of Jesus, and other New Testament writings. Read Chapter 2 as background.

4. Introduce the *oikos* concept, showing its relation to Israel, its importance in the New Testament, and its implications for the church today.

C. *Teaching Plan*

1. Personal sharing with one other person on the question: "By whom has your life as a Christian been affected/influenced/shaped, and in what ways that you can identify?"

2. Recap of Session 1.

   a. What we did and why; samples of "My Current Understanding of Stewardship" and discussion.

   b. Brief lecture on "Christ as Center"; how reflected in our lives? Draw material from Chapter 1 of this book.

3. Purpose, objectives, goals, expectations for this session — leader and participants.

4. Mini-lecture on the *oikos* concept (see especially *God's Stewards* by Brattgard), and group response.

5. Encounter with reading related to this session.

   a. Feedback on reading done since last time. Questions, thoughts, comments.

   b. Small-group (two to four persons) study of scriptures. Look for the one big idea that has significant bearing on the topic.

   Genesis 1:26-31; 2:4b-9   Luke 19:1-27
   Creation   Zacchaeus and Pounds

Psalms 24:1-10	Mark 10:17-22
The Lord's	Rich Man
Micah 6:6-9	Matthew 25:31-46
Do Justice	Last Judgment

c.   Sharing in total group on results of Bible Study.

6.   A look at Session 3.

Suggested readings: Luke 12:13-21; Luke 12:41-48; Luke 16:1-9; Luke 21:1-4. Chapter 2 of this book.

SESSION 3 — "Life Is the Stuff of Stewardship" (cont.)

A. *Purpose:*   Pursue further the focus on life in all its aspects as the way we do stewardship.

B. *Objectives for the Session:*

1.   Provide opportunity for persons to indicate concerns, any mid-course suggestions.

2.   Show film, *How Good Life Can Be* (available from denominational stewardship offices) and discuss how it relates to the topic for the session.

3.   Engage in total group Bible study of passages that illuminate the topic.

C. *Teaching Plan:*

1.   Opening moments — The Lord's Prayer, brief meditation by leader or class member, and silence.

2.   Review of what the group has done so far; list on chalkboard.

Fix the *oikos* concept in the group's thinking.

3. A look at where we are and where we want to go.

   a. Group's evaluation, suggestions for improving the sessions, and other ideas.

   b. Leader's purpose and objective for the session; group's feedback.

   c. Comments growing out of reading during the week.

4. View *How Good Life Can Be* (approximately thirty minutes).

   a. In groups of three, discuss the following (divide the time so that each person has a chance to share):

      1. What happened to you as you viewed the film? How did you feel?

      2. What crossing points did you find with the theme for Sessions 2 and 3?

   b. Brief sharing in total group.

5. Group discussion: What do we mean when we talk about *life*? Is it the stuff of stewardship? If so, what are the implications? See pages 25-27 of this book.

   a. Consider the holistic approach vs. compartmentalization. Illustration: Brother Lawrence.

   b. Ask participants to provide examples of the holistic approach to stewardship in their own words, from their own experiences and relationships.

6. Responsibility is a condition of life for human beings. Agree or disagree? Why?

7. Brief lecture and discussion on life as translated into:

   a. Time — everyone has same amount; how used? who is at the center of it?

   b. Talent — natural abilities and developed skills; used for whose purposes and toward what ends?

c.   Treasure — stewardship deals with all, what we give away and what we use in other ways; proportionate giving concept; tithing; the importance of making a will.

d.   Trash — concern for the earth, environment, ecology, energy; God's risk in placing the earth and its resources at the disposal of humans.

e.   Tissue — many of us can give life through donations of blood; stewardship of body after death through donation of body organs or entire body for research.

f.   A whole host of other concerns: our influence, successes, failures, hardships, thinking, feeling, speaking, listening.

8.   Total group study of 2 Corinthians 8:1-15 and Luke 12:13-21.

Questions: How would you have felt as one of the original recipients of Paul's letter? How did the writer feel? What do these passages mean for us today?

9.   A look at Session 4.

Suggested readings: Luke 20:9-16; Matthew 5-7; 1 Corinthians 12:4-11; Ephesians 4:1-16; Vernard Eller, *The Simple Life*; Wallace Fisher, *A New Climate for Stewardship*; Chapter 3 of this book.

SESSION 4 — "Stewardship Is the Bodying Forth of Theology"

A. *Purpose*:   Work at developing a proper sense of our identity as stewards of God in keeping with the biblical record.

B. *Objectives for the Session:*

1.   Introduce *oikonomos* and *oikonomia*, and develop the

concepts, building on the previous study of *oikos* (Bratt-gard) and the material on pages 29-32.

2. Provide opportunity by means of Bible study and discussion for the group to work further on its understanding of stewardship.

3. Deal with the topic.

C. *Teaching Plan:*

1. Opening sharing, review, general comments, feedback from reading.

Brief quiz on the first three sessions. Purpose is to sharpen thinking and generate discussion (quiz follows on pages 113-114).

2. Group study of Ephesians 4:1-16 and 1 Corinthians 12:4-11.

a. Write in one sentence your paraphrase of the major idea of each passage.

b. Have you experienced or observed the kind of relationship described in these passages?

c. Do you see how you fit into the body? Do you see how others in this group fit into it?

d. Relate these passages to the topic for this session.

3. Mini-lecture on *oikonomos* and *oikonomia*; see pages 30-31.

a. Consider the English words and their meanings: steward; manager; custodian; housekeeper; trustee; agent; administrator. What do these have in common?

b. See dictionary definition of steward.

c. Refer to passages where *oikonomos* and *oikonomia* are found.

Luke 12:42	Romans 16:23	Galatians 4:2
Luke 16:1-3	1 Corinthians 4:2	1 Peter 4:10
Titus 1:7		

4. Opportunity for unhurried discussion on stewardship as an expanding idea and stewardship as relationship.

5. Mini-lecture on theology.

   a. Meaning of the word.

   b. All of us are theologians; see pages 32-33.

   c. How keep stewardship practical? What specific actions are you taking?

6. A look at Session 5.

   Suggested readings: *Journal of Stewardship* (see Appendix A, number 8) for information and inspiration; Matthew 25:14-30; Ephesians 3:1-13.

A FAITH VIEW OF STEWARDSHIP

A Review Quiz to Sharpen Thinking and Generate Discussion

(1-4 are true/false statements; place a check in front of the T or F.)

1. ____ T ____ F   Stewardship and creation are closely related in the biblical view of things.

2. ____ T ____ F   Stewardship is a New Testament concept exclusively.

3. ____ T ____ F   Stewardship in the biblical sense is usually confined to money.

4. ____ T ____ F   One's stewardship is a purely individual matter that has no relation to membership in the Christian community.

5. The biblical approach to history can best be described as (a) cyclical; (b) linear; (c) vertical (please circle one).

6. *Oikos* is a Greek word used in the New Testament which means (a) house/household; (b) barn; (c) carpenter (please circle one).

7. Which of the following meanings of time most accurately reflects the biblical notion of time?

   ____ a.   clock or calendar time that is concerned with the measurement of hours, days, and years.
   ____ b.   content, events—what happens within calendar time.

8. Stewardship is concerned with _____ percent of one's possessions, resources, life.

9. In what ways would you say Christ is the center of life?

10. How would you describe in one sentence the holistic approach to stewardship?

SESSION 5 — "Practical Theology Is the Language of Faith"

A. *Purpose:*   Attempt to correlate the practical implications of stewardship with the theological language of faith.

B. *Objectives for the Session:*

1. Review the meanings, relationships, and significance of the three Greek words studied thus far: *oikos, oikonomos, oikonomia.* Review all of Chapter 3.

2. Introduce the topic for the session and discuss the practical implications of living as a steward.

C. *Teaching Plan:*

1. Initial sharing from the week's experiences, reading, reflection. Look briefly at Matthew 25:14-30 and Ephesians 3:1-13.

2. Review *oikos, oikonomos, oikonomia*; Chapter 3 of this book.

3. Discuss the relationship between creationist theology (identify) and stewardship.

   a. Look again at Creation stories.

   b. What happens to self-centeredness for persons whose lives are centered in Christ?

4. Small group (four or five persons) consideration of the place of *things* in the Christian's life.

   a. Should one get along with as few things as possible?

   b. Should one enjoy the things that are here? Feel guilty?

5. Sharing with the total group concerning number 4 above (refer to Martin Hengel, *Property and Riches in the Early Church*).

6. Concept of vocation; stewardship of daily work, pages 32-35.

7. Consider in silence: "As an individual, how do I relate our discussion about stewardship to my own life?" Be specific.

8. Group conversation in response to communion with one's self, followed by one-to-one conversation.

   a. How do we develop our theology, our own word about God? The Bible, childhood training, parents, family, friends, thought, study, prayer?

   b. Recall and describe persons whose belief and actions in reference to stewardship were/are tied together.

   c. Do you agree that our lives are the true indication of what we believe? That the values we hold and the commitments we have are projected on the screen of life?

9. A look at Session 6.

   Suggested reading: Scan the Book of Acts; read Chapter 4 of this book.

SESSION 6 — "Faith Is God's Gift to the Church"

A. *Purpose:* Work on what faith is, especially as God's gift to those who belong to the body of Christ.

B. *Objectives for the Session:*

   1. Engage in depth study of 1 Corinthians 12:12-31a for the purpose of seeing clearly the importance of the body and each of its members.

2. Consider the meaning of faith and its place in the Christian's life; draw on material in Chapter 4.

3. Review the Greek words again; add a new one.

C. *Teaching Plan:*

1. Review the last session's discussion and material dealt with in all previous sessions.

2. An in-depth study of 1 Corinthians 12:12-31a. Leader should be prepared to provide commentary, with group entering into discussion.

3. Write in a sentence or two your understanding of the word "faith."

   a. See Hebrews 11 for a summary of persons of faith as viewed by a Christian with deep appreciation for his heritage.

   b. Consider the meaning of "faith" and "belief." Draw on your own thinking and check it with the dictionary and with other members of the group.

   c. Note that faith goes beyond the intellect; it depends on, implies, assumes a relationship. Illustrations from your own experience.

   d. See "Illustrations of Faith" section of this book, pages 39-41.

4. Review again *oikos, oikonomos, oikonomia.*

5. A brief study of 1 Peter.

   a. Look especially for evidence of *oikodome* (being built up as "living stones" into the wall of God's house); see also Brattgard, pages 26 following.

   b. To be *edified* is to be built up within the company of God's people.

     c.   Note the relational approach to stewardship in this epistle (e.g., 1 Peter 2:1-10). See pages 37-39 and 41-43 of this book and "The Church as Christ's Body" section, pages 45-48.

  6. A look at Session 7.

     Suggested readings: Matthew 28:16-20; 1 Corinthians 4:1-7; your denomination's official statement on stewardship; Chapter 5 of this book.

SESSION 7 — "The Church Is God's Servant in the World"

A. *Purpose:* To see the stewardship role of the church as God's servant in light of the Great Commission, and to bring the study unit to a conclusion.

B. *Objectives for the Session:*

  1. Discuss the church's proper role as steward of the gospel; see how mission fits in; read Chapter 5 of this book.

  2. Consider your denomination's statement on stewardship.

  3. Examine local church practices in stewardship.

  4. Bring the course to its conclusion.

C. *Teaching Plan:*

  1. Discuss: What connections can be made between the Great Commission (Matthew 28:18-20) and the Book of Acts within the context of this session's topic?

     Ponder and discuss Emil Brunner's assertion that the church exists by mission as a fire exists by burning.

2.   Mini-lecture on mission, money, membership.

   a.   Mission starts where we are but reaches out to where
        we will never be; pages 48-50 of this book.

   b.   Consider per-capita giving; income; inflation.

   c.   What of the view that "the next great revival in the
        church may come not by numerical growth but by
        subtraction" (quoted in Briggs, *Theological Perspective of Stewardship*, page 123)?

3.   Consider your denomination's official statement on
     Christian stewardship (can be secured from denomina-
     tional stewardship office). Does it fit with the emphasis
     of this course?

4.   Discuss the four marks of a financially successful church
     (see article by George M. Siudy, Jr., in *Journal of
     Stewardship*, Vol. 29, pages 21-26):

   a.   The pastor's attitude; see Chapter 6 of this book.

   b.   The congregation's morale and trust; see Chapter 7
        of this book.

   c.   Year-round education; see Chapter 7 of this book.

   d.   Systematic commitment enlistment; see Chapter 8 of
        this book.

      1.   Do you agree with these four marks?

      2.   Do a group inventory of how your own congrega-
           tion measures up.

      3.   What should be included in a year-round pro-
           gram of stewardship development?

5.   Summarize where this course has gone by means of a
     quick review.

6.   Write a statement of your theology of stewardship,
     recalling the description of theology as an activity in
     which all persons of faith participate (see thought-starter
     sheet on page 121 and read Chapter 2 of this book).

7. Fill out written Questionnaire and Course Evaluation (see page 123). Engage in group sharing.

8. Parting words: "This is how one should regard us, as servants of Christ and stewards of the mysteries of God" (1 Corinthians 4:1).

A STATEMENT OF MY THEOLOGY OF STEWARDSHIP

The following may be helpful as you formulate your statement:

1. What is your view of God? How do you describe God?

2. What is your understanding of stewardship? How far does it reach and how much of life does it touch? How is it related to your word about God—your theology?

3. What place does Jesus Christ have in your theology?

4. Recall the characteristics of a good *oikonomos*.

5. How does stewardship fit into your own Christian faith? Is it a cause or result of commitment?

6. Do you see implications in stewardship that are both individual and corporate?

7. Does the view of life as a "pilgrimage in relationship" help? See Romans 14:7,8; Psalms 24:1.

Name _____

A FAITH VIEW
OF STEWARDSHIP

Questionnaire and Course Evaluation

1. Indicate in a few sentences your perception of the term "holistic stewardship," and distinguish it from a fragmented or compartmentalized approach.

2. Write a one-sentence statement on the meaning of each of three of the following words: a. *oikos*; b. *oikonomos*; c. *oikonomia*; d. *oikodome*.

3. List three characteristics of a good steward: a._____; b. _____ ; c. _____ .

4. Write a brief paragraph about your understanding of stewardship in the Old Testament and its relationship to the New Testament idea.

5. ____ Yes ____ No. My attitude as a Christian steward toward things and material possessions has changed during this course. If yes, in what ways?

6. ____ Yes ____ No. Do you feel you have grown in your understanding of stewardship during the last six weeks? If yes, please identify specific areas of growth.

7. On the following scale, indicate your feeling about the *content* of the course.

Very good _____ Very Poor
   1   2   3   4   5

Comments: _____
_____

8. On the following scale, indicate your feeling about the *methods/approaches* used in the course.

Liked   Did
very much _____ not like
        1   2   3   4   5

Comments: _____
_____

9. I found the sessions to be (please circle one) a. Somewhat tiresome; b. Fairly interesting; c. Stimulating; d. Very exciting.

10. I found the opportunities for personal involvement with others during the course to be (check all that apply):

____a. Bothersome; straight lecture would have been better.

____b. Necessary in order to keep my attention focused.

____c. More demanding than I had anticipated, but helpful.

____d. A means of developing my understanding of stewardship.

11. I did none/some/most (please circle one) of the suggested readings for *at least two* of the sessions.

12. What suggestions would you offer for improving the course?

SELECTED BIBLIOGRAPHY

Baum, Gregory. *Man Becoming*. New York: Herder and Herder, 1970.

Bennis, Warren. *The Unconscious Conspiracy: Why Leaders Can't Lead*. New York: AMACOM, 1976.

Bonhoeffer, Dietrich. *Christ the Center*. New York: Harper and Row, 1966.

_____. *Ethics*. New York: Macmillan Co., 1970.

Brattgard, Helge. *God's Stewards*. Translated by Gene J. Lund. Minneapolis: Augsburg, 1963.

Briggs, Edwin A., ed. *Theological Perspectives of Stewardship*. Evanston: General Board of the Laity, Division of Stewardship and Finance, 1969.

Brunner, Emil. *I Believe in the Living God*. Philadelphia: Westminster, 1961.

Eller, Vernard. *The Simple Life*. Grand Rapids: Eerdmans, 1973.

Fisher, Wallace E. *A New Climate for Stewardship*. Nashville: Abingdon, 1976.

Jegen, Mary Evelyn and Manno, Brunno, eds. *The Earth Is the Lord's*. New York: Paulist, paperback, 1978.

Johnson, Douglas W. and Cornell, George W. *Punctured Preconceptions*. New York: Friendship Press for Section on Stewardship and Benevolence, National Council of Churches of Christ in the U.S.A., 1976.

Lawrence, Brother. *The Practice of the Presence of God.* New York: Fleming H. Revell, 1895.

Murphy, Nordan C. *Christians Doing Financial Planning.* N.p.: Commission on Stewardship, National Council of Churches of Christ in the U.S.A., 1972.

_____. *Commitment Plan Handbook.* N.p., 1973.

Richardson, Alan, ed. *A Theological Word Book of the Bible.* New York: Macmillan, 1951.

Rolston, Holmes. *Stewardship in the New Testament Church.* Rev. ed. Richmond: John Knox, 1963.

Thompson, T.K., ed. *Stewardship in Contemporary Life.* New York: Association, 1965.

Webster's New World Dictionary. Cleveland and New York: World, 1968.